Holy Old Whistlin'

YARNS ABOUT ALGONQUIN PARK LOGGERS

BRENT A. CONNELLY

Published by

GSPH GENERAL STORE
PUBLISHING HOUSE

499 O'Brien Rd., Box 415, Renfrew, Ontario, Canada K7V 4A6
Telephone (613) 432-7697 or 1-800-465-6072
www.gsph.com

ISBN 1-897113-34-X

Printing by Custom Printers of Renfrew Ltd.

Printed and bound in Canada

Cover design, formatting and printing by Custom Printers of Renfrew Ltd.
Excerpt from *The Road Home*, by Roy MacGregor and published by General Store Publishing House, has been
used with permission.

Library and Archives Canada Cataloguing in Publication

Connelly, Brent A., 1939-
    Holy old whistlin' : yarns about Algonquin Park loggers / Brent A. Connelly.

ISBN 1-897113-34-X

1. Loggers--Ontario--Algonquin Provincial Park--History--Anecdotes.
2. Algonquin Provincial Park (Ont.)--History--Anecdotes. I. Title.

FC3065.A65C66 2005   634.9'8'0922713147   C2005-906363-7

Table of Contents

Cover: *Algonquin Park loggers enjoying a working lunch*

Brent A. Connelly

Holy Old Whistlin'

Dedication

This book is dedicated with love to my wonderful wife Heather;
our children Janet, Michael, Brent, Christine, Kathy, John, and Nancy;
our grandchildren Matthew, Ryan, Courtney, Amanda, Alexa-Rae,
Deborah, Christopher, Justin, Daniel, Hannah, and Nicole;
and the generations to come.

Introduction

"The snow was axle-deep to a Ferris wheel, so we had to shut down the logging operation and go home."

—Unknown Algonquin Park Logger

Much has been written about Algonquin Park, and the book stores at the park's visitor centre and logging museum offer a multitude of choice on subjects ranging from its fauna, flora, and geology to its rich human history. It is such a special place that for many just one or two visits may be enough to arouse the spirit in an attempt to capture its beauty and impression in words and pictures.

I am privileged to have been a part of Algonquin's human history for twenty-nine years, ending with my retirement in 2000, having been employed as a professional forester on logging and forest management operations throughout that beautiful place. Ontario's other provincial park crown jewel, Lake Superior Park, was my workplace for another nine years in a "dream come true" career in forestry. During those thirty-eight years, I have known and worked with so many unforgettable characters that the little voice inside me, which has guided me so well throughout my lifetime, has given me an ultimatum: "Share it with us, Old-Timer. At the very least you owe it to your family and perhaps others who may be interested. If not, you will toss and turn every night for the rest of your life."

Add to that the old chestnut, "books will beget books." In his book, *A Life in The Bush—Lessons from my Father*, well-known Canadian author Roy MacGregor talks about his father's life and about the relationship they shared with each other. I, too, had a relationship with Duncan MacGregor when we worked together in the early sixties for McRae Lumber Co. at the Rock Lake Sawmill in Algonquin Park. I was the rookie forester starting my first real job. Dunc was the seasoned bushman with a heart as big as Opeongo Lake.

As I read the book, he came to life in my mind. I could see him walking over to the sawmill with a tally book under his arm, his black rubber boots rolled down a couple of inches from the top, a white hard hat perched over a red wool liner covering red ears in the wintertime. I saw him leaning back in an old chair at storytelling time in the mill office after supper and hear his wheezy laugh, and the tch . . . tch . . . tch . . . exclamation of disapproval or surprise in the midst of, listening to, or telling a story. Yes, Roy had brought his father back to life, and for me it was an opportunity to have one last visit with him.

After reading the book I e-mailed Roy, whom I had never met but knew much about. I told him that his dad was my friend and how much I had enjoyed the book. I also included some anecdotes about Dunc and others at Rock Lake that he would not have heard before. He responded quickly and thanked me for sharing the stories with him. He also suggested casually that "perhaps some day you may want to write your own book."

The seed had been planted. After receiving much encouragement from my wife Heather, within days I had completed a list of many of the colourful characters with whom I had worked over the years. There were loggers, lumbermen, truck drivers, bulldozer operators, timber cruisers, foresters, cooks and cookees, rogues and rascals—enough human interest fodder to fill Cole's and Chapters to the rafters. What a perfect opportunity it would be for me to bring those old friends back into my life for one last visit, like the one I had with old Dunc!

The cast of these remarkable characters is so extensive that a single book could not introduce them properly. This book is about some of the Algonquin Park loggers and lumbermen I have known. The rugged loggers from the Highlands of Algoma will be left for another day, and perhaps another book.

So there you are! I was now compelled to do something. There was no need to overload the space occupied by the many previous accounts of the romance of the early timber barons and their workers. Instead, I have attempted to fill what may be a possible void and tell you about some of the men I worked with during the last half of the twentieth century. I will leave it to others to discuss the forest management, political, environmental, and industrial aspects of forestry activity in provincial parks. I have focused on the human side with emphasis on the humorous—it was more fun that way. Serious and more accomplished historians than I can capture the other stuff.

This is a varied collection of odds and ends about these people, their personalities, tough work ethic, on- and off-the-job antics, humour, and wisdoms. Yes, there is embellishment here, but it was at the knee of some of these men that I learned to tell the stories. However, the anecdotes are all true and will be told with as much accuracy as my memory will allow.

The loggers and lumbermen I have known were deeply proud individuals and inclined on most days to be profound and profane when talking about their work. I have tried to moderate the profanity as much as possible, at the same time recognizing to exclude it altogether would be like painting a picture of a rainbow and leaving out a colour or two.

This was a culture where a "boardroom" meeting was two or more men huddled over a map splattered with dead blackflies, spread out over the hood of a half-ton truck. The "minutes" of the meeting consisted of a few numbers scratched on a Buckingham cigarette package.

"Doing lunch" was sitting on a log alongside a colleague sharing a story and a cup of tea made from loose tea leaves and boiled over a fire started from a dry, white pine stump. A head cheese and mustard sandwich topped off with a thick slab of cheddar and a slice of onion on homemade bread would be toasting on the end of a forked stick, an opened can of beans would be warming in the coals. Dessert was a squashed half of a raisin pie with date squares on the side.

A "conference call" was two truck drivers screaming over the CB radio at another driver, "Pull over onto your own side of the road, you son-of-a-bitch, or we will pin your ears to the bunkhouse door when we get back to camp."

"Dressing up for work" was to waterproof a pair of boots or put a wool liner inside a hard hat and add another pair of socks when winter arrived.

"Payment for goods and services" was not via high-speed electronic Internet transfer. It was quite often a bartered arrangement, a load of firewood for a skidoo trailer, a side of moose for an old chainsaw. Cash was not frowned upon as it is today. A friend of mine once sold some fuel wood to a jobber and was paid through the open window of his half-ton truck with $10,000 in cash in a green garbage bag.

A "9-1-1 medical emergency call" was not help coming around the corner in five minutes. Instead, it could be a four-hour agonizing wait with a broken back, strapped to a stretcher under a tree, before the ambulance arrived. In later years it was a hundred-mile trip to the hospital in an air ambulance helicopter. I once drove a man seventy miles from a logging operation to a Sault Ste. Marie hospital with his nose cut in two from a chainsaw kickback. He was passing out so I had to tie him to the passenger door to prevent him from slumping to the floor. One spring, a logging foreman, bush mechanic, and I transported a critically injured logger out of the bush to seek medical attention. He had been struck by a falling tree and was lying unconscious on a stretcher. During the trip, the crew bus that we were travelling in became stuck in a mudhole for several tense and frantic moments. We were out of radio range and were unable to call an ambulance to meet us until we reached the highway. Sadly, he died two weeks later.

"Relaxation after supper" wasn't sitting mindlessly in front of a television set or chatting on a computer with a cave dweller from Borneo. It was men sitting around the bunkhouse or foremen's shack telling stories to each other until the 9 p.m. snack in the cookery and the generator was shut down for the night. The stories were about logging, hunting and fishing adventures, families, truck drivers, bar-room fights, women and mythical wilderness monsters, and were, for the most part, wonderfully unforgettable. There was laughter and wonder, embellishment and lies aplenty. The imaginations had no limits.

At times the quips and exaggerations flew wildly like sawdust from the end of a screaming chainsaw.

Brent A. Connelly

Holy Old Whistlin'

A bulldozer operator from Whitney once told us, boastfully, "I mind the time, on a forty-below day last winter when I was bulldozing roads in Lawrence Township, I froze my willy. It was too far to go back to camp, so I got off the dozer and rubbed it with snow for as far as I could reach, and snowballed the rest."

One logger while relating a story said, "I mind before I was born." Another, trying to impress listeners with his humble start in life, said, "I was born in a log cabin that I had built myself."

An old Algonquin Park logging foreman was once asked how his sex life was now that he was getting a little older. He replied, "Welllll, I still manage, and it takes me a little longer to get the job done, but I don't begrudge the time."

While it will be necessary to briefly outline some of my personal background to explain what brought me to Algonquin Park in the first place, I hope that you will enjoy hearing about these remarkable characters, who touched my life and the lives of so many others.

Chapter 1—Shaping a Dream

"Count your life by smiles, not tears—Count your age by friends, not years."

—Bits & Pieces

Dreams were plentiful growing up as a boy in Brownsburg, Quebec, a small town of 2,500 in the Lower Ottawa Valley. After listening to Doug Smith's play-by-play radio broadcast of the Montreal Canadiens on a Saturday night, I would fall asleep, seeing myself streaking down left wing in the Forum in overtime of a sudden-death final Stanley Cup game against the Leafs. Elmer Lach would snap me a crisp pass. In an instant, it would be in the top corner of the net, past a sprawling Harry Lumley to win the Cup. Alas, it was not meant to be, and the closest I came to the Stanley Cup was obtaining an autograph from Jean Beliveau, when he came to referee a hockey game in our town.

There were many other such fantasies but, with maturity, I turned toward more realistic dreams. As I reflect on my life and my work career in these retirement days, the realization is there in boxcar letters: I have fulfilled an amazing dream! I obtained a Bachelor of Science degree in forestry from the University of New Brunswick and became a professional forester, and worked in the forests of Ontario's Algonquin and Lake Superior Parks for close to four decades.

Bill Brown, former general manager of the Algonquin Forestry Authority (AFA) and a colleague of mine for twenty-five years, and I were having lunch one beautiful fall day on the shore of the Bonnechere River. We had spent the morning visiting some contractors in Algonquin Park on a tour of active logging operations. As we started the small fire to boil water for tea and to toast our sandwiches, we sat there gazing out over the quiet serenity of the gently flowing river. While shaking our heads, we remarked to each other, "Imagine, we are actually getting well paid for this." There were many days over the years when I had similar feelings, although on days spent snowshoeing in blinding snowstorms or fighting blackflies in the middle of some godforsaken swamp in late afternoon, ten miles from the truck, the feeling would diminish somewhat.

There are two parts to a reflection on the last fifty years in Algonquin Park—the forests and the people. Foresters are trained to manage the establishment, growing, and tending of forests. They are driven by a host of socio-economic objectives, including timber production, wildlife habitat enhancement, air and water quality protection, and recreational opportunities, to mention a few. Today, foresters accept a total integrated resource management responsibility.

I am proud, and can attest to the fact, that the forests of Algonquin Park are in much better condition today than they were fifty or one hundred years ago. Then, the primary reason to invest or work in the forests was to produce timber for commercial purposes, the recognition of other dynamics and values being secondary or non-existent. Currently, in zones where logging is permitted, operations are on a cycle that allow the return to the same area every twenty years in perpetuity.

The increase in awareness for all that the forest contains and supports has been very dramatic over the years, both in the professional and public domains. It is with amazement and sadness that I reflect on an example of this.

In the early 1960s, in the southern regions of Algonquin Park, Ontario Department of Lands and Forests officials asked the logging crews to burn all dead pine trees (chicots) as they encountered them during cutting operations in winter months. These massive trees were considered to be forest-fire hazards due to their lightning-strike potential. They were ideal habitat for a variety of small mammals and birds as they contained numerous cavities. I vividly recall snowshoeing on hilltops, looking down over snow-covered slopes and valleys, and seeing these towering candles burning against a blanket of snow. The forest landscape resembled a giant birthday cake, and to see flying squirrels fleeing the safety of their forest home was heartbreaking.

Present-day management practices provide maximum protection for these trees. Tree markers strive to identify them and create buffer zones for their protection.

As mentioned earlier, I will leave the successful park forest management story to be presented in the volumes of technical reports, management plans, audits and public reviews. Instead, I will focus on the human side of the story, which is also an excellent statement and measurement of forest sustainability. While serving as acting general manager of the AFA in 1999 and 2000, I wrote the following for the general manager's report of business for that year:

> The turn of the century is an appropriate time to reflect upon the sustainability of the forests of Algonquin Park. Modern foresters have sophisticated methods to assess and demonstrate forest sustainability. Elaborate growth and yield and wildlife data sets feed into complex computer models which analyze and grow forests electronically through future decades. The results are impressive and indicate a very positive future for the Park's forests and are consistent with results from independent Forest Audits.

> There is another way, however, to demonstrate forest sustainability in terms which all of us can relate to, and that is in human terms. The forest industry is the lifeline of many small communities surrounding the Park. Ongoing milling operations such as the 3rd generation Murray Bros. Lumber Company in Madawaska, the 4th generation McRae Lumber Company in Whitney, and the 5th generation Herb Shaw

and Sons Lumber Company in Pembroke, stand as real examples of the sustainability of the forests of Algonquin and adjacent regions.

Last winter a young professional logger from Barry's Bay named Steve Glofcheskie was employed as a logging foreman in the Odenback area of Algonquin Park. In the 1970's his father, Gilbert Glofcheskie, was also a foreman for Hogan Lake Timber in the same area, and in the generation before that his grandfather, Tony Glofcheskie, was employed in the same forest as a logging superintendent. Several other family members have also been employed on logging operations in Algonquin over the years. Steve has a very practical knowledge of the dynamics of the forest and, combined with the experience of his family, confidently states that, "The continuation of current forest management practices in Algonquin Park will ensure forest sustainability for the benefit of many future generations."

Most of these men were true bushmen. They lived, worked, and played in the bush. A vacation was a time to be away from work, but to be in the bush to enjoy the deer or moose hunt. This culture resulted in logging and sawmilling operations commonly shutting down for a week in the fall to allow fathers to take their sons out of school and give them a real education at the hunt camp. Danny Janke, currently AFA operations manager in Pembroke, once told me with joy in his face that "the hunting season was better than Christmas."

As a small boy, the anguish of tying or wearing a necktie was painful. Wouldn't it be great to have a job that didn't require fussing in front of a mirror in the morning? Yes, it has been great. In thirty-eight years I have probably only had to wear a sports jacket and tie to work a handful of times. However, since the pattern of work consisted of a combination of office and fieldwork, often in unpredictable order, it was always best to have the boots and mackinaw close at hand.

Occasionally, my wife Heather would try and dress up her little boy to go to work, but usually without too much success. And she sure wasn't pleased with an impression I once made while working for the AFA in Pembroke.

Our office was on the second floor of an old school next to the local welfare office. One day, while going up to our office, I met several people coming down from the welfare office. As we passed on the stairs, one lady looked at me, stopped, and suggested, "There is no use going up there now, your cheque won't be ready until this afternoon."

"The only things that trees cannot do that humans can do is sprint the one-hundred-yard dash and play a flute."

—Mansiel (Manny) Wilson, forester and woodlands manager

My journey to Algonquin Park began when I was fifteen and my father, George Connelly, took me to meet his boyhood friend and track-and-field teammate, Mansiel Wilson. He was a graduate forester and worked as a woodlands manager for the Canadian International Paper Company (CIP) in Grenville, Quebec. He was responsible for supplying the raw material to a sawmill in Calumet, Quebec, and a pulp mill across the Ottawa River in Hawkesbury, Ontario. Mansiel was also instrumental in establishing the Harrington Tree Farm, which still exists today, producing tree seedlings for planting and regeneration programs in the forest industry. The facility was also a renowned demonstration and research forest for the development of hardwood forest management systems. Mansiel was the central figure in all of this.

My father recognized the prominence of his old friend and introduced him to me knowing that I would be impressed and helped by what he could tell me of his career in forestry. To say that I was impressed would be a huge understatement. I was in awe of this man for many years. Later on in my career, I read about his work and met him several times at forestry conventions and seminars. He was a pioneer and leader in the forestry profession.

Mansiel Wilson: "I don't talk to the trees, but I sure listen to them."

When we entered his large office, he was sitting at a huge oak desk, with wood burning in a large stone fireplace in the background. I was struck by his black bushy eyebrows, his welcoming smile, and the extension of a friendly but firm handshake to a mere wisp of a boy. As a bonus, he was wearing bush boots and a plaid shirt, without a tie. The walls were covered with wildlife paintings and pictures of trucks and bulldozers; a slide rule sat on top of an orderly pile of papers on his desk. A disc cut from a maple tree to show the annual growth was nearby.

Through the large window, I could see his mud-splattered company half-ton truck in the parking lot. In my mind, it was there for him to jump into and drive up to Harrington on a nice day, whenever he tired of office work. It couldn't get much better than that!

We were in his office for about two hours and the phone didn't ring once, nor were we otherwise interrupted. My father took notice of this and remarked on the way home that Mansiel had probably given instructions to his secretary to take messages. Mansiel talked at length about his job and the reasons for his choice of career. The thing I remember most, however, was his great love for the forest. He loved trees and commented about the common life-support systems that humans share with trees.

I have often thought of these commonalities, especially when travelling alone in the bush. Some examples of these processes are birth resulting from the fertilization of female flowers, followed by juvenile development, competition for space, sun and nutrient, maturity, disease, healing of wounds, and mortality. Trees have respiratory and circulatory systems, and it is known that diseased trees will have increased temperatures.

Some foresters will chat the ear off you, espousing the existence of a rudimentary nervous system. It is very common for trees to react to stress through prolific seeding or foliage deterioration. I have observed this on many occasions. There is a tree species in South America which, when threatened, will excrete a strange substance from its foliage. This is considered by some observers to be a warning to its neighbours of an impending insect infestation. There are many other such examples— a very interesting subject indeed!

I was to learn much from Mansiel, probably the most important being his effort to make time for a young, wide-eyed boy. I strongly believe that if I had arrived at his doorstep, unknown and without my father, I would have had the benefit of the same reception. Throughout my career, I have tried to replicate his example when visited by a young person seeking guidance, by shutting everything down and taking whatever time necessary to chat. In later years, voice mail sure helped with this. It is my hope that, somewhere, there may be someone who was helped by me, as I was by my first "real-life" forester and hero, Mansiel Wilson.

I guess Mansiel thought he would check me out after our first meeting. I found myself with a summer job at the Harrington tree farm before going away to the first year of university. In the beginning, there were assorted jobs, such as thinning tree plantations, counting gravel trucks, and killing pigs for the cookery. I stayed in the tree farm headquarters camp on the Rouge River and would hitchhike home every two weeks. The facilities were elaborate, with individual bedrooms, a huge rec room with fireplace, and a state-of-the art cookery—almost resort-like. It was used frequently for forestry conferences and retreats and was very much unlike some of the beetle-infested logging camps I stayed in later on.

And then it happened, on a June afternoon! The day that I am sure opened the door on my career in Algonquin Park. I was about to embark on one of the most exciting adventures of my life. My foreman, Ernie McRae, came to me and asked with a smile, "Do you know how to swim, lad?" With eagerness, I replied, "Sure, I know how to swim. My parents have a cottage on a lake, and I have been in the water all my life."

"That's good," he said, "because tomorrow you are going to start working on the Rouge River log drive. You are going to be a log driver. Today you are a sixteen-year-old boy—tomorrow you may become a man. Be sure and get a good sleep tonight, you'll need it." I didn't sleep a wink that night. I was on the eve of manhood!

The Rouge River has its headwaters in the Mont Laurier region of western Quebec and flows into the Ottawa River at Calumet. Each winter, CIP had its logging contractors pile logs and pulpwood on the river's edge. In the spring, the timber was released down the river, destined for the mills at Calumet and Hawkesbury. It is a wild and beautiful river and currently supports several commercial rafting operations. It had many falls, rapids, eddies, and above-surface rock outcrops, which presented obstacles to the free passage of the wood. Logs jammed up on these features and were stranded high and dry on shoreline beaches. Sweep crews began in late April in the upper reaches of the river and moved through to where the Rouge met the Ottawa River, recovering this material, to allow it to float downriver. They had riverboats and a portable tent camp set-up with a cook. The operation took most of the summer to move downstream over the full length of the river.

It was very dangerous and physical work, with the experienced men working out of boats on the edge of the log jams, usually on the lip of falls or rapids. They would find the key logs, which supported the jam, and pull them free with their long pike poles. Others would spend the whole day in the water, pulling logs away from the shore and out into the main current. Some beaches were plugged with logs and debris and, in many cases, this material had to be manhandled into the water.

The Gatineau Boom Company was ordinarily contracted by CIP to sweep the river, but because there was an unusual amount of wood hung up that year, coupled with a shortage of men, crews at the tree farm were called upon to help. That is how my opportunity came about.

The next morning I was up before our cook had rolled out of bed. I remember his bleary-eyed surprise when he met me waiting for him in the cookery. We were to be trucked to the river, leaving at 6:30 a.m., and I wanted to be ready. I began to make my lunch, as we normally did, and he teased, "Today you become a man so you can expect to have a real working-man's lunch. It will be an all-you-can-eat luncheon buffet supplied by the drive cook." Boy, did I have a story to tell that old bugger when we arrived back that night for supper.

Ernie dropped us off on the shore of the river with the drive crew. We were in the river fully clothed, up to the waist in water and pulling on our pike poles before 7:30 a.m. There were six of us from the tree farm, including myself, Howard "Please-and-Thanks" MacLean, Willie Diamond, and Harvey Campbell. The water was very cold with the ice floes barely out of sight, but I was so excited it didn't matter. I was happier than a pig in popcorn! There were about thirty-five men on the job, mostly French-speaking. Most of us were in the water all day, while the foremen and a handful of the more experienced men worked out of three wooden longboats. They may have been the well-known pointer boats of Pembroke fame, I'm not sure. If they weren't, they were good replicas. They were rowed with two or three sets of large oars and the bow and stern were pointed.

Around 10:30 and feeling a little hungry, I looked for signs of the "working-man's lunch" that I had been told about. Since their breakfast is so early, men working in the bush normally have their lunch at 11 a.m. so I knew it would be along anytime. At 10:45, the old foreman jumped on shore, chopped some driftwood, and made a fire. He cut a tea pole and hung a huge pail of water on it for the tea, but still no sign of the lunch.

A few minutes later, a boat appeared from upstream carrying a large wooden box. The foreman took it ashore and opened the lid and yelled, "*Viens ici.*" Next came the loudest warhoop I had ever heard, as thirty-four men flew out of the water and swarmed over that box, like wolves tearing at a deer carcass. They were coming away from the box with armloads of bread, chunks of meat, and cakes. I could hardly wait, but lingered a bit to drain the water out of my boots. When I got to the box, I could see it was divided into three compartments lined with yellowed newspaper. There was meat in one compartment, and bread and cakes in the other two.

I couldn't believe it. It was almost empty. Where was my all-you-can-eat feast, the meal that was going to make a man out of a boy?

My lunch that day consisted of a stale molasses cookie, the heel of a piece of homemade bread and a small chunk of fat, scarcely boasting a trace of pork, which I washed down with five or six cups of potent tea. Still hungry, my thoughts turned to supper back in our own cookery, as I walked back into the water for the afternoon.

Ernie McRae and our old cook back at the tree farm camp were right about me becoming a man that day. The following day, I had my elbows up before I hit shore and was near the front of the pack arriving at the lunch box. I couldn't wait to tell him that night that I had finally had my "working-man's lunch."

It was an awesome summer with every day serving up a new section of the river. It didn't matter if it rained, because we were wet anyway, and on beautiful days it was like a vacation. One sunny day we were working near the small community of Bells Falls, on the upstream side of a hydro dam. There was a huge log jam in the middle of the river about one hundred feet from the spillway, where the water tumbled over to the rocks below. The foreman and two other men climbed into a boat, which was secured to each shore with large ropes tied to the bow and stern. On each shore, a crew of men controlled the boat by wrapping the rope around large pine trees. I was on one side, gripping so tightly to the rope that my hands became sore. The men picked away at the jam with their pike poles for what seemed an hour. Finally, the logs were released over the dam. It was a dangerous and exciting experience. If my dear mother had come along at that time, she would have had the whole log drive shut down before the water for tea had boiled.

At one time during this operation, I glanced down to the beach and saw a group of tourists and cottagers gathered to watch and take pictures. They greeted us cheerfully when we made it downstream to the beach. There were some girls my age in the group, so when the men went into the local hotel for a beer, I stayed on the beach to demonstrate my river-driving skills to them. By that time the old-timers had taught me to walk on and ride floating logs. The girls were impressed by that and took more pictures. I couldn't help but think about some of my chums back home who didn't have jobs and were cavorting on the beach showing off to the girls—and here I was getting paid for it. It was a good day!

Mansiel Wilson also showed up to take our pictures that day. He was probably out for a little spin to get away from the paperwork.

The next summer, I was employed by CIP in its Maniwaki division, having been interviewed by a company representative on campus. Once again, I found myself working on a log sweep. This time it was the Baskatong Reservoir, which is a huge body of water created by flooding the Gatineau River for hydro-electric generation. Company crews swept the shores, freeing up timber to float downstream to mills at Gatineau.

We met Indian families as we worked along the shoreline. They lived in tents, having left their permanent communities for the summer fishing season. Most of them had limited knowledge of both English and French. One day, as we were working on a remote shore of the lake, we came upon a small church built on a beautiful sandy point. It was a log structure containing hand-hewn pews and a crude pulpit. At the front of the church was a plain, clear glass window, with a small piece of broken stained glass fitting into a bottom corner. It was easy to imagine the thrill that someone felt when they found that piece of glass.

Five or six of us sat quietly in the pews for a few minutes with our own thoughts. It was a spiritual moment for me. On a trip to London, England, after my retirement, we lucked into having communion in Westminster Abbey. That was an unforgettable experience also, but could never match the few minutes that I had in that little church on the Baskatong.

The drive crew was entirely French-speaking, and the only word that the foreman could speak in English was the command "backwater." He shouted this when directing the boats.

The camp was built of unpeeled logs, and since I was the youngest, I was assigned to the top of the three vertical bunks. My bed was about eighteen inches from the rafters—a nose-length away from the sound of the beetles chewing on the logs. There were forty men in the one-room bunkhouse and, at night, I would wake up to a chorus of snoring. Many men woke up at night to smoke, and you could see the glow of cigarettes throughout the room. It was like sleeping in a sawmill with a background of Christmas tree lights.

The camp was powered by a small generator, which could only support limited refrigeration. This meant that if we had pork chops and potatoes for supper, we could expect to have the same for breakfast, along with bacon and eggs. It was really something to see a man start his day with a plate full of eggs, pork chops, turnip, and sugar pie.

The community toilet that we used was called the jay bar. It was a small makeshift building located behind the bunkhouse. Inside was a half-peeled spruce pole about ten feet long, which was positioned horizontally over a five-foot-deep ditch. On some parts of the pole, knots were not cut flush to the surface, thus creating a few sharp protrusions. Understandably, this was the section of the pole not commonly used. At arm's reach above this there was another pole, slightly smaller.

The trick was to sling your carcass over the bottom pole and hang onto the other pole—and believe me you hung on. To slip off the jay bar would be disastrous. Reading a newspaper in a configuration such as this was out of the question, although there was always someone sitting next to you to chat with.

There was one member of our crew who didn't fit in. He was a university student, a couple of years older than me, and was the son of a high-ranking CIP executive. He clearly had an aversion to work. He also had an attitude problem towards the culture that he found himself in. He complained constantly about many things, including being wet all the time, the recycled food, and the jay bar.

There must have been an incident that the rest of us didn't know about. One night after supper, when we were relaxing in the bunkhouse, the old foreman came storming through the door. He kicked the end of the guy's bunk and shouted angrily at him, "*Prens le pacsac et vois le commis*." Translated, this meant, "Get your packsack and go see the clerk." The supply truck was in camp at the time, and they shipped him out to Maniwaki that night. We never saw him again. As it turned out, he was probably the luckiest one of the crew. He would have danced in the streets had he heard what was to happen next.

Personal hygiene in this camp setting was deplorable by any standard, with the possible exception of the trenches of Vimy Ridge. Cold water in tin basins at one end of the bunkhouse was used to wash up in the morning. A skinny dip in the lake on a Sunday afternoon was the weekly scrub-down. Our clothes barely dried out during the week, as we were in the water most of the time.

After four weeks in the camp, we began to notice that about every second man was regularly scratching his ass in an agonizing manner. Finally, the whole crew was affected by some form of exotic rectal infection, and the camp was shut down temporarily. I had to go home and lie in the bathtub for about three days and take penicillin.

I recall that trip home vividly. I hitchhiked from Maniwaki and became stranded along the road in the middle of the night without a ride. I spent the night sleeping under a tree near the road, outside the village of St. Canut, with my packsack as a pillow.

When I returned to Maniwaki the next week, the drive camp had still not reopened. I was given another assignment, which provided me with the opportunity to work with two seasoned bushmen. I was teamed up with Norm Baird, a CIP forester, and Vital Turcotte, a forester employed by Gillies

Bros. Lumber Company. Our job was to freshen up old axe-blazes on the trees, which designated the limit line between the timber licences held by the two companies. We covered a lot of ground and travelled mainly by canoe and foot. It was a very remote area and we stayed in trappers' cabins or abandoned logging camps near lakes, where possible, to enable a pontoon plane to fly in food supplies weekly. Bologna was the "catch of the day" when we didn't have time to fish for fresh speckled trout.

One stifling hot day, we were stopped in the middle of a dense black spruce swamp, spitting out blackflies, and not quite sure of our location. The landscape was very flat and there were very few prominent topographic features to guide us. Norm and Vital were huddled over a map trying to get a bearing with a compass. I can recall Norm remarking, "If we go north, we won't come across any landmarks until we hit James Bay. We don't have enough bologna to take us that far."

Once we were staying in an old logging camp and sleeping in the foreman's shack. We ate and kept our food in the dilapidated cookery, which was not very secure. One night we heard some noise coming from the cookery and, upon investigation, discovered that a bear had ripped down a door. He ate a week's supply of tubed bologna that was hanging from the rafters. We lived on speckled trout, sardines, and canned tomatoes for the rest of the week until the plane returned.

The next day, before going to work, we patched the door and Vital rigged up an innovative spring pole arrangement at the same door. It had cans tied to it and was intended not to harm the bear, but to give it a swat on the nose and create enough noise to scare him away. It worked, because during the night we heard a commotion and peeked out the window to see the hind end of the bear running for the hills.

In later years there were many other such bear encounters involving break and entry into camps and cookeries. AFA tree markers working out of a batch-trailer at Hogan Lake were dismayed to return to the trailer, hungry and tired after a hard day in the bush, to find it completely ransacked. The door of the propane fridge had been ripped off and the empty fridge was on its side.

In 1999, Dane Brown, an AFA tree marker, was chased by an aggressive bear before his courageous dog finally frightened the bear off. Jeff Driscoll, an AFA forest technician, was also challenged by a bear in the park interior, and while running to his truck threw down his hard hat. The bear hesitated a few minutes to mangle the hat, enabling Jeff to reach his truck safely. Jeff recovered the hat afterwards and brought it in to show me. It had been torn into little pieces, with teeth marks quite visible. I had it in my office for a long time as a reminder to everyone of the potential danger of bears. Many bushworkers now working in remote areas carry canisters of pepper spray and, where possible, are teamed up with co-workers.

After two summers working for CIP, in 1958 I moved on to Eastern Forest Products Laboratory of Ottawa—and Algonquin Park, where I worked the next three summers before graduating from the forestry program at the University of New Brunswick.

This was a federal government research facility focused on the practical development of forest products, such as plywood, wood particle products, and laminated wood construction timbers. I worked for the wood utilization section, and we travelled extensively to at least twenty logging and sawmilling operations throughout Ontario and Quebec.

We had projects in Algonquin Park at the Staniforth Lumber Company operation in Kiosk and on the Hay & Co. operations in southwestern regions near Tea Lake. I became obsessed with the majesty of Algonquin Park, and the dream was set. I knew that I had to return there to work on a full-time basis.

Under the direction of experts such as Frank Petro, Bill Calvert and Tom Imada, we conducted time-and-motion and product-value studies in logging and sawmilling operations. Logs were measured and graded in the bush and followed through the mills. Each board was measured and graded at the output end of the mill. This enabled a value-recovery analysis to be made, providing company management with hard data on the effects of log quality and manufacturing methods on their bottom line. Frank Petro eventually wrote a book, *Bucking for Profits,* outlining some of the findings. It has been widely used in the hardwood forest industry as a training resource.

The forest industry was experiencing much difficulty during my graduating year of 1961, and permanent job prospects were limited. It seemed that government jobs were practically non-existent as well, with the exception of the Alberta Forest Service, which attracted several of my classmates. However, my sights were set on Algonquin Park, and I couldn't shake it. I obtained a directory listing all the forest industry companies and government agencies in Canada and over the winter wrote to all of the ones located east of the Manitoba–Ontario border. Many of the letters were not even acknowledged; the others said, "We regret that there are no job openings at this time."

To this day, I have a great deal of empathy for young people seeking employment. I was always impressed by Joe Bird, who was the first general manager of the AFA. Much like Mansiel Wilson, he would ensure all applications were acknowledged, while frequently including a few personal words of encouragement. He set a great example for all of us in so many ways.

Discouragement began to set in during brief periods of temporary employment after graduation in 1961. Slinging cement on a high school construction job in Lachute and working in the lab for a plastic dome manufacturer in St. Andrews East seemed light years away from fulfilling my Algonquin Park dream.

Chapter 2—McRae Lumber Co. Ltd.

"Fire the son-of-a-bitch. The only work he is doing around here is making debt for me."

—J.S.L. McRae, Owner of McRae Lumber Co.

And then it happened! One night after returning home from wheeling cement all day, there was a letter. It was from McRae Lumber Co. of Whitney, Ontario. They apparently still had the letter I had written to them the previous year. Alex MacGregor, McRae's clerk, told me later that mine was the only letter they had received. That is why I was contacted. I was at the top of the list in a field of one.

They wanted me to come to Whitney for an interview, "as soon as possible." Within minutes, I had called and arranged to be in Whitney for 9 a.m. the following Saturday. The interview was to be with J.S.L. (Jack) McRae, the owner, and his son Donald. I didn't get any sleep that night, as I kept asking myself what "as soon as possible" meant. Was my dream finally going to come true?

I had only four days to do some much-needed research on McRae Lumber. I knew nothing about the company or the area other than I had passed through Whitney when working with Tom Imada. We had stopped for ice cream cones.

I called Frank Petro and a few others and learned that Jack McRae had started in the lumber business as a young man with his father, who had owned a sawmill and grist mill in Eganville. He moved to Whitney and purchased an existing sawmill on the shore of Galeairy Lake, and operated it until it was destroyed by fire. He then constructed a sawmill at Lake of Two Rivers, a short distance south of the present-day campsite, having obtained a licence to harvest timber on Crown land in Algonquin Park. Subsequent to the wind up of this mill, he built another one at Hay Lake, a few miles south of Whitney. This was followed by the construction of the current mill in 1962 near Rock Lake in the park.

This mill was a modern, double-cut band mill, which produced six to eight million feet of lumber each year. The production consisted primarily of high-quality hardwoods, such as maple and birch. There was a complete camp facility at Rock Lake, as well as logging camps constructed in the bush, as required. The company also owned considerable deeded land south of Whitney. More than one hundred people were employed by the company, many of them of Polish descent, and the mostly full-time workers alternated between the sawmill and logging operations.

Jack and Donald McRae were highly respected in the lumber industry and were regarded as successful, astute, hard-nosed lumbermen. I would have to be up for my game on Saturday!

I left after the late show on Friday night, arrived in Whitney before 7 a.m., and had breakfast at Greg Larochelle's Shell station. A few of the locals in the restaurant gave me a curious, who-the-hell-is-that look as I sat there enjoying my bacon and eggs. I was slicked up a bit with a neat sports jacket and freshly polished shoes. But no tie.

I was later to discover that Greg's was the town's hangout and meeting place. If you needed to know anything or find anyone, you would find the answer there. They also served the best and most original club sandwiches known to man, made with fried egg and ham. I have eaten hundreds of them over the years.

I had some time to spare so I drove around the town of 900 residents, who were mostly of Polish ancestry, but I couldn't find McRae's sawmill or office. I finally returned to the Shell station to ask directions and chatted with the boys for a few minutes. They were pawing at the ground to find out who I was and why I wanted to find Jack McRae so early on a Saturday morning. They told me that his office was in Airy township about a mile west of town; the sawmill was at Rock Lake in Algonquin Park.

I drove to Airy and found a huge white clapboard house situated on a hill overlooking Galeairy Lake and the abandoned right-of-way of J.R. Booth's Ottawa, Arnprior & Parry Sound Railway. It was distinguished by a large full-length verandah facing the lake. Close by were several other smaller but neatly kept houses. They were all that remained of a community that had depended on the former railway and a McRae sawmill, which had burned.

It was in one of these houses that well-known author, journalist, and media personality, Roy MacGregor, first peeked out over the sides of his cradle. He talks about his early life at Airy in the book about his father and describes how his mother "had three babies at once in cloth diapers, and no running water, no electricity, and no help."

I looked around, but the only sign of life was a man stooped over splitting kindling behind his house. His dog was lying close by, not even looking up as I walked around the yard waiting for nine o'clock. A rooster could be heard in the background, and a couple of kids were fishing off the old railway trestle at the narrows. It was very peaceful, but I was shaking like a leaf.

There were a couple of cars parked at the big house, and at one end of the building was a small finger sign indicating "McRae Lumber Co. Ltd." At five minutes to nine I stepped onto the verandah and started looking for a door to knock on. The first door I came to appeared to be the office. I peered in a window and saw what looked like an old man sitting with his back to me, reading.

He opened the door and told me to come in. He didn't introduce himself or ask me who I was. He just sat down on a chair beside an old beat-up desk and stared up at me. On the desk was a pile of papers and trade magazines and a jar containing short wooden pencils. (It would not be too long before I would discover the magic that those pencils could perform.) The room was dark and smelled of stale cigarette smoke. A large pendulum clock on the far wall ticked softly, but with authority.

The old man was smoking a cigarette that boasted a one-inch ash and was wearing a pair of high-topped laced dress boots, a plaid shirt with no tie, and an old cardigan sweater darned at the elbows. We chatted a bit about the weather and he grumbled something about "The goddamned tourists will be coming in a couple of weeks. It will be like being on Highway 401 driving into Whitney."

J.S.L. McRae, "the boss."

For the next five or ten minutes, I leaned on a counter that separated us and wondered, "Who in blazes is this old guy? He must be the clerk or the caretaker."

The old man finally told me to sit in a chair facing him and began asking me a few general questions. Then he asked, "What does your father do?" It suddenly hit me. This had to be Mr. McRae. It was time to bear down and be alert. I thought, "But why in hell is he asking what my father did?" My father had a job—it was me he should be asking about.

I was surprised he didn't have my résumé in front of him. Eventually, he got around to asking me what kind of work I did in the bush. Can you scale logs? Can you travel in the bush without getting lost? Can you find a gravel pit? Not one question about my university education—that was of no interest to him. I told him about my experience working in sawmills throughout Ontario and Quebec.

And then I hit the jackpot! I explained that I had been a log driver, and when I described how I had fought and scrambled for my "working-man's lunch," an approving grin came over his face. We had struck common ground. For the balance of his interview with me we talked about the river drive. How thankful I was at that moment for having known Mansiel Wilson.

That was it—the end of the interview as far as he was concerned. Mr. McRae picked up the phone and called his son Donald to come meet me and drive me up to the mill to look around. There were no more questions. Then he proceeded to tell me why he was hiring a forester— and how he felt about having to do that.

He had previously employed an old Polish forester named Felix Tomaszewski. Felix also did work for Murray Bros. Lumber Company of Madawaska under a shared arrangement and had started preparing a three-year operating plan, when he suddenly died. The plan had to be submitted to the Ontario Department of Lands and Forests before the end of the year. Their approval of this plan was a prerequisite for granting authority to McRae to harvest timber on Crown land for the following three-year period. The pressure was on.

McRae explained that he didn't need nor did he want to hire a goddamned forester. "Those government bastards have me by the throat," he growled. "I have a camp full of good bushmen at Rock Lake who know all there is to know about cutting timber. Imagine! They are telling me I have to hire a son-of-bitch of a forester to write a plan. All it will do for me is to make me more debt."

However, the job wasn't mine yet. As Donald drove me up to the mill, he fired off some sharp questions to determine my level of experience, particularly in hardwood forestry, and the scope of my education. Plus, how did I feel about bringing my family to live in Whitney?

McRae "board meeting," from left to right: unknown, Gary Cannon, Duncan MacGregor, J.S.L. McRae, and Edward Kuiack.

How did I feel? I was twenty-three years old, married with two young kids and, as is often the case when people marry too young, things were not going well. Bringing home a steady paycheque would surely help, wouldn't it? I felt fine, I told him.

We toured around the mill and the camp. I met Frank Molo, the old Polish chore-boy, who made the camp his full-time home. Gary Cannon and Bob Shalla were running the log peeler over the weekend, preparing for mill start-up on Monday morning. We missed Duncan MacGregor that day. He was in his boat, coaxing the fish out of Whitefish Lake.

When Donald and I returned to Airy, we went into the McRae residence, which was in the same building as the office. I was asked to sit in the parlour as father and son went into the kitchen, carefully shutting the door after them. In a few minutes, they came out, and Donald told me that I had the job. "Four hundred dollars a month and free room and board when you are staying at the camp. We want you to start a week from this Monday." He added, "There is no housing available in Whitney for your family right now. You will probably have to rent a place in Huntsville and commute until something becomes available."

Then Mr. McRae chipped in, "And you can be sure that since there is not enough work here to keep a forester busy full-time, we will have lots of other things for you to do. We may have to teach you how to drive a log truck or a bulldozer," he chuckled. McRae was a man of his word, I soon learned.

When I left Whitney that afternoon I was on top of the world. Dreams do come true! I had landed my first real job in forestry and would be working for real lumbermen and in Algonquin Park. It didn't matter that my new employer was only hiring me because "a bunch of bastards had him by the throat."

I stopped at the Balmoral Hotel in Barry's Bay for a cool Dow, a chunk of kielbasa and a pickled egg, and whistled "Dixie" all the way home. Wow! What a day it had been!

The following Monday was a sunny day. I arrived at Rock Lake with my compass, a new pair of boots and a packsack full of books, ready to work and eager to learn. It was June 1962.

To describe the cast of characters that I was to work with over the next three years, I have to start with J.S.L. McRae, whose initials stood for John Stanley Lothian. He was called "the boss" or Jack by the men at the mill, with the exception of Eddie Pencoskie and myself. We called him Mr. McRae.

Mr. McRae was an intelligent, shrewd, self-made lumberman as tough as a two-dollar steak. He was sometimes obnoxious, oftentimes stubborn, most times feisty, and all times in complete control of his company. And when the sun went down and nobody was looking, there was an ample supply of kindness, thoughtfulness, and compassion.

He would think nothing of throwing the radio out of the window, if he didn't like the weather forecast. I was told he once did this during a winter log haul at the Hay Lake mill while listening to the 6 p.m. news. The report was not what he wanted to hear, and when the cookery bell rang for supper, he heaved the old wooden radio through a window. He then kicked it to the cookery door, leaving a trail of splinters, tubes, and wires scattered all over the yard.

He had the most astonishing ability to "follow the dollars" of anyone I have ever known. Those stubby little pencils would add up a column of numbers in an instant—and the bottom line better not be negative. God did not put us on Earth to make debt! I am certain he had an outside source supplying him with those pencils, as I didn't once see him use a full-length pencil.

His capacity to be aware of the smallest detail of his operation did not take away from his attention to and control of the big picture. The art of delegation was not in his bag of tricks, although he relied heavily on decisions made by key men, such as his son Donald and his brother-in-law Duncan MacGregor. Some of his methods would have driven modern-day management experts out of their minds, but it worked for him and it worked for us.

Logging foreman Paul Kuiack was once building a logging camp near Lemon Lake. Mr. McRae, who was ordering the supplies for Paul, asked me to drive him up to the camp one fall evening. He wanted to take measurements for stove pipes to be installed in the cookery to service the wood-burning cook stove. It was dark and there we were, the two of us, on our hands and knees under the light of a coal-oil lantern. We were each holding the end of a tape to measure for an order of stovepipes, probably amounting to a value of about $15. And, of course, he recorded the measurements with his stubby little pencil.

The reason this memory has stayed with me all this time is that before that week was out, I witnessed a sales agreement and a cheque he wrote on the spot in the Rock Lake mill office for $125,000. He handed it to an International Equipment sales representative for the purchase of ten TDC–5 skidding tractors, and added, "I know where to find you, if those goddamned things don't do the job."

That contrast between the two items of business was striking—dinghies on Monday, ocean liners on Tuesday.

Mr. McRae normally worked in his office at Airy, but would drive up to the mill two or three afternoons a week. He would stay for supper and visit with his old friend Tommy Cannon, who was our cook. After supper, he met with his men to conduct business in the mill office before driving home. Those were interesting evenings involving mill-yard and lumber-shipping foreman Duncan MacGregor, logging walking boss Sandy MacGregor, logging foreman Paul Kuiack, and clerk and scaler Paddy Roche, and anybody else who might wander in, or be summoned.

I was included in those bear-pit sessions for the first ten months, as my family was now living in Huntsville. During this time I was only able to get home on weekends and occasionally Wednesday nights. The rest of the time, I stayed in a room at the rear of the mill office. I cherish the memories of those evenings, filled with stories and wild yarns.

Sometimes the business discussions heated up to the point where a chair would get kicked over, or somebody would stomp out the door to cool off for a few minutes—but always to return. Mr. McRae eventually purchased a house in Whitney, which he rented to me, and I would drive back and forth to the mill with Donald each day. I missed those evenings at Rock Lake.

Mr. McRae had a two-way radio in his Airy office. The second one was in the mill office, and he would frequently be on the radio to whomever was in the office at the time. The radio system apparently was not subject to any monitoring from regulatory third parties. The result was the common use of fairly descriptive language.

Normally, the sawmill would operate ten hours a day from 7 a.m. to 6 p.m., Monday through Friday. It also ran until noon on Saturday, making it a fifty-five-hour week. Mr. McRae always insisted that the log haul be completed by mid-February. After that, we would be "making debt." The logging operations worked five days, but during the log haul the standard was "whatever it took." Truckers worked fourteen-hour days and commonly on Saturdays, although I can't remember ever having to work on Sundays. For most, that was the day to attend mass in the big church on the hill in Whitney. For some, it was a storytelling session at Greg's Shell station, and for a few of the high-spirited, an afternoon visit with the "bootlegger."

It was a Saturday morning in February during the log haul after a spell of freezing rain the day and night before. The roads were glare ice, and I was running around frantically with a couple of men in my half-ton truck, sanding bush roads and trying to head off the prospects of making more debt for "the boss." There were sixteen tandem trucks on the haul, and the first truck should have arrived at the mill before 7 a.m. It was 10 a.m. and there was still no sign of the first truck. Many of them were standing by at the bottom of hills, waiting for the sanding crews. Time was money!

I stopped by the office to pick up my lunch, which I had forgotten. As I entered the room, a grinning Duncan MacGregor, who was just leaving, told me that "the boss" was looking for me. I overheard in the background an impatient Mr. McRae shouting on the radio, "CJN819 calling Rock Lake. Answer the radio, dammit it all to hell anyway!" Thinking that he would be asking me about the haul, I answered. I was amazed to find that he was locked on to something else, completely unrelated. I was to learn, starting with that day, that he could be like a bulldog on a root. He would solve one problem at a time and not move to the next one until the first one had been fixed.

Without asking anything about the trucks, he roared, "I am going over some invoices from Canada Packers, and that goddamned Tommy Cannon is making debt for me again. He has gone and ordered that 'yella' margarine. I have told him a thousand times that the 'yella' margarine is a cent a pound more expensive than the white stuff. All he has to do is to put the white margarine in a pail, add the little packet of 'yella' colouring, and stir it with a stick. But he is too damned lazy to do that. That son-of-a-bitch!! Now you go up to the cookery and find out if Cannon ordered the 'yella' stuff, or if Canada Packers is trying to screw me."

I told him that I was sanding roads and that there were no trucks in yet, and asked if it could wait until afternoon. "I want to know now and get right back to me," he replied. I went up to the cookery and, of course, Tommy couldn't find his order. His grocery orders were in a drawer mixed in with packages of yeast, baking powder, and raisins. He was a cook, not a file clerk.

Finally, Tommy said, "Tell the old bastard it was the white margarine that I ordered. And tell him to stick to the lumber business, and not mine. I don't have any time for this bullshit. I have to get back to my cinnamon rolls."

I went back to the office and radioed him with my report. He seemed satisfied and then told me, "You had better get into the bush now and get those hills sanded." The best part of that story was Tommy and Mr. McRae were great friends and would have friendly chats in the cookery during the evenings. It was amusing to hear them snap at each other and shower each other with insults.

Earlier that same day, Dunc, the old bugger, had pulled another classic prank on me, which I will describe later. He was two for two that day. He knew very well that if he had answered the radio himself, it would have been him chasing down margarine orders and not me. Since I was the young newcomer, I occasionally found myself the subject of such practical jokes. It didn't bother me, as I looked upon it as some form of right of passage.

Whenever I tell the next story I think of Harry Searson, who is a successful logging equipment distributor and businessman in Eganville. Harry is well known by most lumbermen and logging contractors in Eastern Canada. He has sold equipment to most of them. I would meet Harry at Fiddle Park in Pembroke during the Old Time Fiddling and Step-Dancing Contest. If there was an audience nearby, Harry would ask, "Brent, tell us the story about you, Jack McRae, and the sweet corn."

When I wasn't timber cruising or working on other forestry-related activities, I would help Paul Kuiack and Sandy MacGregor on the logging operations—laying out roads and checking on the cutting crews. In those days, we had sixteen two-man crews: eight using horses to skid the logs out to the roadside for pick up by truck and eight crews using small skidding tractors. The crews stayed in the camp at Lemon Lake, less than an hour's drive from Rock Lake.

On the way out of the bush each night, I stopped at the Lemon Lake camp to pick up the grocery order from the cook, Harry Rapson. I gave it to Tommy Cannon in the cookery at the mill on the way home. He would have it ready for me to pick up in the morning.

Within a year of starting at McRae's I had become well established. I was living in Whitney and Mr. McRae called me each night about seven o'clock to get a rundown on that day's activity in the bush. I provided him with the log count, who was on the job that day, and what equipment was down for repairs. He was especially interested in Mondays. He wanted to find out who might have been drunk over the weekend and didn't show up for work.

One night, he called me right after supper and asked, "How many men are in the camp at Lemon Lake now?" I informed him that there were thirty. He went on to say, "I bought some fresh corn today from Mrs. Eddie Pencoskie. It is in Tommy's storage shed at the mill. Take up a couple of bushels when you go to the bush in the morning."

At about nine o'clock, as I was plowing through the snow on the single TV channel available in Whitney, the phone rang again. It was "the boss," one more time. He asked, "How many cobs do you think a man will eat for supper?"

I replied, "Probably two or three." He responded, "I am not sure how many cobs are in a bushel. You had better take three bushels up with you in the morning." As I reached for my pocket notebook, I thought, "I hope that old bugger goes to bed pretty soon!"

At about 10:30, the phone rang for the third time that evening. Guess what . . . it was him again. "Brent," he said, "I was just going to bed and telling Mrs. McRae about the corn. She said that when a working man gets his first feed of corn of the season, he will be looking for more of the same the next night. Take the whole goddamned works up, and I will buy some more tomorrow."

Three phone calls over about five dollars worth of corn. How is that for tracking detail? Nothing was going to get away from this man. If only he could have been our federal finance minister for just one day.

I recently told that story to Bob McRae, Jack's grandson, and he matched it with one of his own:

"For many years, the company purchased turkeys for all its employees at Christmastime. My grandfather personally presided over their distribution to the families of the more than one hundred employees. With the help of a butcher's scale, and in a spirit of fairness, he was there when the delivery truck arrived, making sure that the largest turkeys were given to the families with the most kids."

Some modern-day skeptics might call the practice time-wasting micromanagement. They are probably the same people who would arrange to be centre-stage hosts of a gala Christmas cocktail party in a fancy hotel ballroom attended by a few high-ranking executives, standing around clinking glasses, munching on canapés—and admiring themselves. Ask yourself. Who would you prefer to work for? The answer is a simple one for me!

Obviously, there was much more to Jack McRae than monitoring the purchase of margarine, turkeys, stovepipes, and corn. These examples are used to illustrate his attention to even the smallest detail of operating costs. It is not to infer that he didn't have time for the larger, more important items on his robust agenda.

Such was not the case. From my vantage, he covered it all. From his office in Airy, and with the help of his assistant, Alex MacGregor, he presided over the total sales of the mill's production. His customers were long-standing wholesalers who had purchased lumber from him for many years. The sawmill was continuously being updated and was expertly maintained. The lumber was of excellent quality and, under the watchful eye of Duncan MacGregor, was graded, sorted, and shipped to match order specifications.

The lumber was manufactured from high-quality hardwood timber grown on prime sites. The industry standard in those days was for only good-quality trees to be harvested. This was also a reflection of the inadequately developed forest management systems prevailing at the time. Crown harvest regulations applied a generic stump diameter limit to standing timber, resulting in the biggest and best trees being cut. In some cases there were no diameter limits. The outcome was a "help-yourself-to-the-best-and-leave-the-worst" scenario.

Modern-day forest management prescriptions in Algonquin Park require trained forest technicians to assess and designate with paint individual trees for harvest or retention. The criteria leading to these decisions include factors such as health (quality and maturity of the trees), presence of regeneration and old growth, wildlife habitat, competition, site and water quality protection.

In the late 1960s, when these new forest management systems were being introduced, there was an uproar from the loggers and lumbermen. It was a sharp reversal from the previous standard. It was seen as "help yourself to the garbage and leave the best"—a recipe for economic disaster. The diet had changed overnight from filet mignon to bologna.

The reality is, however, that the lumber industry relying on raw material from Algonquin Park has experienced some tough times during this transition period. But the dividends are now beginning to show on the horizon. Improved tree quality, growth and yield, and abundant regeneration will become the new norm for decades to come.

McRae Lumber is surviving this continuum of change. It did so by adapting its manufacturing facilities to match the size and quality of the timber produced from the forest. It was my good fortune to have worked on both ends of this unfolding change. I was able to participate in, and bear witness to, the powerful dynamic of the forest to develop under sound forest-management principles.

During the time that I worked for the company, I was not aware of any occasion when Mr. McRae had to travel away from Whitney to sell lumber. Sales were usually conducted over the phone. Since he was either in his Airy office, having supper at Rock Lake, or chatting at Greg's Shell station, his customers knew where to find him.

He was "hands on" with changes to the mill and mobile equipment. He knew each of his employees by name, as well as their life histories and home situations. The exception was on the logging operations where the cutting and skidding crews did piecework and were often just passing through.

Employees were paid monthly, and Mr. McRae signed the payroll cheques. If he noticed an out-of-town pieceworker underproducing, we would quickly get the word: "Fire the son-of-a-bitch; all he is doing here is keeping a bed warm—working enough to buy a case of beer for the weekend."

Successful businessmen watch for opportunities to maximize the bottom line. Jack McRae had a keener eye for this than most.

He called me one winter evening, the only call from him that night, and asked me to pick him up the following morning. He wanted me to drive him to visit a small temporary contract sawmill operating in the park east of Opeongo Lake.

We arrived at the mill about 10 a.m. and introduced ourselves to the clerk. He was working in a small, one-room, tarpaper shack, which served as the mill office. Mr. McRae asked him if we could look around the mill and where the owner was. We were told that the owner was in the bush checking on the logging operation, and that he would be in for lunch. It would be alright for us to look around the mill, which was operating at the time.

I swear that Mr. McRae either had some insider information, or his scent of an opportunity was kicking in. He knew exactly where to look first. Behind the mill was a huge pile of bark-covered maple amd birch slabwood that had been produced through heavy slabbing practices in the mill. In that era, it was common in small, circular-saw sawmill operations, such as this one, for the sawyer to take off a thick slab from the exterior of the log to get at the valuable clear lumber quickly. The slab would then be transferred to a waste pile and either remain there to rot, or otherwise be disposed of.

We began climbing around the piles like a couple of squirrels, and out came that stubby little pencil. I took measurements, he recorded, and we were both struck by the amount of good quality lumber contained in the slabs.

Finally, the owner arrived and he invited us into the cookery for lunch. He had heard of J.S.L. McRae and was thrilled to have such a legendary lumberman as his guest. The two talked generally about the lumber business, and then "the boss" began his probe. "What will you be doing with that pile of scrap slabwood behind the sawmill?" he asked.

 "Oh," the owner replied, "that's a hell of a problem for me. The Department of Lands and Forests insists that I dispose of the pile before the mill starts up again next fall. Next week, I will have a man and a front-end loader working on burning the piles . . . it will cost me a fortune!"

"Well, isn't that a-son-of-a-bitch of a terror," McRae replied, as he licked up the remains of his warm raisin pie. To my surprise, he dropped the subject cold and started to talk about something else. This apparent indifference contrasted with the way he was smacking his lips when we were taking measurements on the pile. I was puzzled.

As we were getting ready to leave, McRae gazed out over the slab pile, then nonchalantly said to the owner, "You know, I would hate to see you take a licking on that garbage over there. I might be able to take some of it off your hands. How would it be if I send a truck over here to pick up a couple of loads? I will see if I can do anything with it and pay you ten dollars a load for your loader to load my trucks. If I can make use of it, I may be able to take it all."

I thought that the sawmill owner was going to kiss him, he was so happy. "Sure thing, Mr. McRae, sounds good to me. Thank you very much—help yourself," he replied.

I couldn't drive the truck fast enough for "the boss" to get back to Rock Lake. As soon as we arrived, at about 2:30 p.m., he huddled with Donald for a few minutes and then charged directly over to the blacksmith shop. I had gone into the office to work and could see the activity through a window.

In a few minutes, he came out with a couple of men. They began rooting around in a scrap pile behind the shop. Next, waving his outstretched arms, he hailed a front-end loader, which was working in the mill yard. He had the operator pull pieces of an old elevator conveyor (similar to a hay-bale conveyor) over to the side of the sawmill.

A welding machine soon followed and, with sparks flying wildly, the discarded conveyor was operational in minutes. Another man with a chainsaw walked into the mill. Soon afterwards, there was the scream of the saw and a cloud of blue smoke, and a huge hole appeared in the side of the sawmill. Then, the conveyor was installed to feed into the mill through the hole. Andrew Sydock was then commissioned to go to Opeongo Lake to pick up the first load. All this happened before Tommy Cannon had a chance to "drain the potatoes" for supper. It played me out just watching it all.

It was organized so that the slabs would be fed into the mill when the head-saw was down for maintenance or saw changes. Duncan MacGregor told us later that the yield from these slabs was of exceptionally high quality, yielding high-value lumber. The McRae mill eventually consumed all the slabwood from the Opeongo operation. The bottom line was enhanced for both parties—everybody was happy!

I also need to be fair to the small sawmill operator. He was not able to use this material because of the configuration of his mill, not because of his failure to recognize the value of the by-product. The McRae mill, on the other hand, was a more permanent mill, equipped with a modern resaw, and could process the slabwood more efficiently. One man's buttermilk, another man's champagne!

I have often contrasted in my mind how a large sophisticated forest industry company with its modern management methods and vast resources would respond to a potential opportunity such as the one we found that day at Opeongo Lake.

The first step would be a memo sent to a half-dozen specialists and managers summoning them to the boardroom for a meeting. Coffee and doughnuts would be delivered; a secretary would be on hand to take minutes; somebody would be charged with completing a return-on-the-investment calculation, which could only be done after another finalized a marketing analysis, and another investigated the costs involved, while the mill manager examined the potential impact on sawmill productivity. It is likely that the union steward and the safety committee would also need to be consulted, not to mention the guard at the gate.

A date would be set for a subsequent meeting to make a decision as to whether to proceed or not. By that time the whole dammed shooting match would be up in smoke. An exaggeration? Probably not!

Nobody took a vacation at McRae Lumber Co. in those days, except to tack on a day, here and there, around a statutory holiday. This included J.S.L. and Donald. A few would take some time off during the hunting season or at Christmas. In lieu of regular vacations, we received our vacation paycheque by the first of July each year. There would be no complaining about it. That was just the way it was!

I had been there for a couple years when I began planning my first real vacation—a trip to New Brunswick. When I received my vacation paycheque in June, I called Mr. McRae and asked if I could see him.

We arranged to meet at Greg's Shell one evening. I returned the cheque and told him that I would like some time off with pay to take a trip instead.

"A trip?" he asked. "What do you want, three or four days?" I told him that I would like two weeks. "Two weeks!" he gasped, while almost collapsing. *Holy old whistlin' Jesus, are you going to the moon?*"

Gary Cannon, a long-time McRae employee and a good friend of mine, was at Greg's that night. When we would meet in later years, he would laughingly describe how "the boss" reacted after I had left Greg's that night. McRae stomped around grumbling, "Can you believe that, he wants two weeks off with pay. That son-of-a-bitch of a young lad is driving me into debt—by the 'holy old whistlin'.'"

The hard side of J.S.L. McRae is what we all saw everyday. The soft side was not as visible, but everybody in Whitney could tell you about it. There were numerous stories about cash gifts, low rents, and loads of slabwood delivered to families in need.

News travelled fast in Whitney, and he was aware that there were problems at my home. One afternoon, when we were alone in the office at Rock Lake, he discretely raised the subject. He offered to lend me money, without interest, if I needed it. I thanked him but declined, knowing that I would be moving on sooner or later.

I was very fortunate to have commenced my career in forestry with J.S.L. McRae. I learned much from him and have thought of him frequently in the years that followed—especially when there was a story to tell about him. My eyes swelled when I first read an excerpt from Roy MacGregor's book *The Road Home*. He was reflecting on his own children, living in another time:

> I wish they could have seen what it was like when the last of the lumber barons, J.S.L. McRae, died and some of the pallbearers—retired men from the mill all, only a few of them owning jackets—wept as they carried him out to the black car that swept down the hill from the church and out onto Highway 60, most of the village gathered along both sides of the road as if the king had died and God alone knew what would happen next.

At the time of his death, I was working in Lake Superior Park, otherwise I would have been there the day of the funeral. I regret that I couldn't have been there.

Donald McRae was his father's son in savvy and toughness and in many other ways as well. He began working around the sawmills as a young boy, and there is a story that I am sure has been amply embellished over the years, but I will relate it exactly the way that I heard it.

McRae had a sawmill on the shore of Hay Lake, a large lake southeast of Whitney. He also had a couple of logging camps some distance from the lake, but only accessible from the opposite shore, as there were no roads. One summer, Donald, who was a teenager, had the job of ferrying supplies by motorboat across the lake for subsequent transfer to the camps for the winter logging season.

One beautiful summer day, he had a live pig standing up tied in the bow of the boat on a trip across the lake. As most young lads would do, he took off from the mill under full throttle. While gazing back to admire the substantial wake that he had created—whack. He hit and ran over a large boom timber in the water, and the boat capsized.

The pig drowned, and men working on the jack-ladder (vertical conveyor) feeding the mill jumped into another boat and came out to rescue the frightened youngster.

Donald, dripping wet and with his tail between his legs, went into the office to change. He met his father. "What happened to you?" he was asked. "Holy Jeez, Dad," he said, "my boat upset and I just about drowned."

"I can see that," the boss said, "but what happened to the goddamned pig?"

Donald's career in the lumber business was interrupted by his service in the RCAF during the Second World War. He was a crew member of a downed bomber and was in a German prisoner-of-war camp for three and a half years. During that time, his whereabouts were largely unknown to his family back home.

Donald and I drove back and forth from Whitney to Rock Lake regularly, and although he preferred not to talk about that experience, he once told me they were fed a diet of boiled cabbage and bread. He often thought of the scraps that Tommy Cannon threw out of the cookery and how much the bears at the dump enjoyed these feasts.

Francis Conway, an expert saw-filer, recently told me another story about Donald that bears repeating. During the time that Donald McRae was a POW, the Whitney parish priest regularly visited the logging camps. After supper, the men gathered in the cookery for mass. On one of these occasions, Jack McRae was in attendance.

When the mass was concluded, Father Hunt asked if there were any special prayer requests. "Yes," replied Jack McRae. "My son Donald is in a prisoner-of-war camp in Germany. I would like you to pray for him. And pray like a son-of-a-bitch."

Don McRae: "I have work to do—don't have time for that bullshit!"

From a distance, some might speculate that Donald worked in the shadow of his domineering father, "the boss." I didn't agree with that. I saw him as a very capable manager, who was unquestionably in control of all the activity around the mill.

Donald was busier than a tick on a moose, constantly in and out of his half-ton truck, driving from the office to the mill, to the lumber and log yards, to the garage, to the blacksmith shop, and to the cookery and back again. At times, he would be out of his truck before it stopped. Once, it got away on him and ran into a nearby log pile, while he ran frantically to catch up to it.

He was very much his own man and would stand up to his father whenever he needed to. However, he had a quieter and more composed manner. To my knowledge, he was never seen kicking a stump in a fit of rage or throwing a radio out of a window, although it was borderline at times.

One day, I was in the office and Jack was berating Donald over the radio. Jack was ranting that one of his boneheaded, son-of-a-whore truck drivers had not filled out a bill of lading properly on the delivery of a load of lumber.

Donald leaned back in his chair and listened for awhile, responding with an occasional grunt and "ten-four." Finally, he switched the radio off, left the office, jumped into his truck, and drove over to the mill. As he walked by me, he said with a little grin, "I have work to do—don't have time for that bullshit!"

Donald had great vision and foresight, and was always very progressive in seeking out new methods and equipment. (Salesmen would often go to him rather than to Mr. McRae for fear of getting the boot.) For example, when the 1974 Algonquin Park Master Plan stipulated that the Rock Lake mill be closed and the site rehabilitated, Donald and his two sons, Bob and John, commenced construction on a state-of-the-art mill complex in Whitney. The complex now consists of a conventional-log sawmill, a small-log sawmill, and a pulp-chip processing plant. It is recognized as one of the most efficient hardwood mills in Eastern Canada. John and Bob, who now manage the operation, field requests for mill tours all the time.

In the late nineties, Bill Hubbert, AFA's Huntsville Area Supervisor, and I were touring a group of sawmillers and private sector and government foresters from Nova Scotia through some of our

Brent A. Connelly

Holy Old Whistlin'

operating areas in Algonquin Park. We included a tour of the McRae mills in their visit. They were pleased to have the opportunity, as they had heard of the operation.

John, J.S.L.'s grandson, led the tour. At one point someone asked him how the current lumber markets were. With a twinkle in his eye and a little grin that I had seen before in another generation, he replied, "The lumber business is terrible—may have to charge admission for these tours to keep from making debt." Holy old whistlin' . . . it was déjà vu all over again for me.

I have been fortunate to have worked and done business with so many sawmillers throughout my career. A partial list includes Jack, Donald, Bob, and John McRae; Dowdall, Gerry, Terry and Ted Murray; Johnnie, Donald, John, and Dana Shaw; Phil and Steven Cooper; David Noik; Grenville Martin; and Bennie Hokum.

These are some of the finest people that I have ever known. However, without exception, they share one common characteristic—one that has provided me with either amusement or challenge, depending on the circumstances of the day.

It can be summed up this way. On any given day, a lumberman will tell you there has never been a good day in the lumber business, "not since Noah went on a shopping spree to build his ark."

Log prices are too high, lumber prices too low. Productivity is too low, interest rates too high. Inflation is too high, return on the investment too low. Log yard is a sea of mud, can't see the lumber yard for dust. And on and on. "Swing Low, Sweet Chariot, Coming fo' to Carry Me Home!"

Lumberman Dowdall Murray, of Murray Brothers Lumber in Madawaska, was once told the following by a young "wannabe" lumberman: "You know, Dowdall, I have sawdust running through my veins." Dowdall replied gruffly, "You had better get yourself a transfusion as soon as possible, or you will die."

These lumbermen would have an outward appearance of success and prosperity. However, when I would arrive to negotiate a log sales agreement with them, they would put on an act that implied the debtors' prison wagon was expected to arrive at the door at any moment to haul them away.

Somebody once suggested a guiding principle for use when negotiating with a lumberman: "Consider the preamble, then divide by two and take off fifty percent."

It was fun—most days! And at the end of it all, Algonquin Park values were protected, sales agreements were concluded, timber was cut and delivered, lumber was produced and sold, and mortgages were paid. Little babies were fed, clothed, and loved. And life went on. What more needs to be said?

This discussion takes me back to Pembroke and Jack Court's barbershop. If you are ever in Pembroke, need a haircut, or even if you don't need one, but would like to have your spirits lifted, be sure and visit Jack's shop on Mary Street.

Jack Court's Barbershop, Mary Street, Pembroke: "Pay for the trim— yarns and lies are free."

The best time to go there is when there are five or six old fellows waiting for their turn in the chair. It is no fun having to go to the chair directly. At times, the shop echoes with a staccato of wonderfully exaggerated stories. Patrons, overcome by laughter, commonly need help to the chair when it is their turn for a cut. However, anyone entering the shop with a ponytail or rings dangling on their face or ears risks being scalped and carried out on a flat board.

I was in the chair one day when Jack asked me how the lumber business was. I had just come from a head-knocking log sales session with Johnnie Shaw of Shaw Lumber. He had softened me up a bit, as he often did. In a moment of weakness, I told Jack that "the mills weren't producing lumber, only debt."

I could see his little grin in the mirror as he reached for a smoldering cigarette in the ashtray on the shelf. In those days, the non-smoking section in Jack's shop was along the far wall where his customers sat. The smoking section was a three-foot radius around the chair where he worked.

Jack then proceeded to tell me about a customer of his, an old farmer from Micksburg named Wilfred. I am sure this same story has been told about thousands of farmers over the years, but this was his version.

Wilfred was chronically complaining about how poorly he was doing in the farming business. He was in the shop one day and Jack asked him, "What kind of a year did you have, Wilfred?"

"It was a regular son-of-bitch, Jack," he replied. "Couldn't get onto the fields in the spring, it was so wet. Summer was so dry the hay wouldn't grow. And beef prices are lower than they have been in years. Me and the wife are going to have to eat seed potatoes this winter to stay alive."

A year or so later Wilfred came in to have his hair cut after a remarkably good farming season. Jack said to him, "The weather was great this year—lots of sunshine and warm rain to make the hay

Brent A. Connelly

grow—and I understand the beef prices are up, too. You must have had a good year, Wilfred," he remarked.

"Wellllll," Wilfred replied. "It was fair-to-middlin', Jack. But you know, a year like that takes a lot out of the land."

"You mean to tell me that you have a university education and that is all you know about the Jacobite rebellion? . . . tch . . . tch . . . tch."
—Duncan MacGregor, logger and lumberman

Jack and Donald McRae were my employers. Duncan MacGregor was my friend.

Duncan's sister, Janet, was married to Jack McRae, and Dunc had worked for McRae's for many years. Duncan was the only man, with the exception of Donald, who could effectively stand up to Jack when he was having one of his rants.

My feelings for Duncan went beyond respect to admiration and affection. He was more than just a simple man who had worked and lived a lifetime in the bush. He was also a fisherman, an intellectual, a storyteller, a philosopher, a teacher, a humorist, a charmer, a poet, an historian, and a baseball junkie. Duncan MacGregor was the kind of man that books are written about, and his son Roy did just that.

Duncan studied books and he studied people. He could talk your ear off with intelligent commentary on current, past, and future affairs. And all without the benefit of a daily newspaper—or the eleven o'clock television news—or even a decent radio. The old wooden radio that sat on a table in the corner in the office was probably a sister of the one thrown out the window at Hay Lake. It could barely pick up a few bars of "The Orange Blossom Special" from WWVA, Wheeling, West Virginia, on a Saturday night.

His vast knowledge certainly did not come from extensive travel. Other than accompanying his brother-in-law J.S.L. McRae on an annual week-long junket to the Canadian Lumberman's Association convention in Montreal, he rarely left Eastern Ontario. But he did read books. There were tons of them—under his bunk, on top of his bunk, and in his packsack. The books were everywhere! When he wasn't telling a story or listening to one, he had his nose in a book.

It didn't take Duncan long to figure out that I was an eager young rookie with much to learn. He recognized that I would be needing some help from him to get started off on the right track. I was always grateful that he took me under his wing.

It also didn't take me long to figure out that I would be no match for his amazing intellect. My background was science. His knowledge was more widespread to include history, geography, the arts, and politics—and he wasn't shy to put an upstart kid with a university degree to the test. He would have me spellbound, as a few of us sat around chatting in the office at Rock Lake in the evenings before turning in for the night. Duncan was a master storyteller, and I can still picture him sitting in the corner, leaning back on that old chair with the broken rungs. The room would light up when his rough yellow and black thumbnail ignited a wooden match to light a giant roll-your-own cigarette. With tobacco spilling over his shirt and onto the floor, the blaze from the end of the cigarette reflected on his smiling, reddish face, which boasted a week-long stubble.

He would frequently preface a statement or editorial comment with, "You know yourself."

"You know yourself, Brent," he would say, "that goddamned czar had it coming, the no good son-of-a-bitch."

Two other McRae's men, brothers Maxie and Bob Shalla, had a variation of Dunc's preface: "Honest to God, you know yourself, Brent," after which it was anybody's guess what sort of a yarn would unfold.

One of the first things that Dunc did was to prepare me for working with the Polish workers at the mill and on the logging operations. "They are fiercely loyal to the company and 'the boss,' and you will never find harder working men than these lads," he told me. "But they are very suspicious and guarded around newcomers. Since it is not often that outsiders move to Whitney, they will be watching you like a hawk. You are going to have to work hard to get them on your side."

He was dead-on with that advice, and it took me a while to break the ice with some of them. After a few months, one of the men lamented to me that he was having difficulty preparing his income tax form. I offered to do it for him, at no charge, and this led to me doing returns for a few others. I wasn't a tax expert by any means, but the men were working for nominal wages and most had few investments, so it was quite straightforward and simple for me to do.

One of the Polish workers was Eddie Pencoskie, a bubbly little man with a big smile. He was the other half of the McRae sweet-corn supply, with his wife splitting her time between the garden and catching speckled trout from the small creek down the road from their house. Eddie was a long-time McRae employee and sorted lumber on the boardway at the end of the mill. He had a heavy Polish accent and called me "Mr. Blent." He couldn't get his tongue around the "r" and insisted on calling me mister, which made me feel a little uncomfortable at first.

Eddie was an active trader in the penny-stock market. If I was in the office during the day, he would sometimes ask me to call his broker in Toronto with an order to buy or sell some shares, or "sherries" as he called them. This was in the days when a call could be made from one location and charged to another.

In the evenings and on weekends Eddie cut hair in his home, a little house on top of the hill in Whitney. He had a barber's chair in his living room and there was always someone in it. From time to time "the boss" showed up for a trim. I have often told my kids, when reflecting on the "good old times," that I could get a good haircut from Eddie for thirty-five cents and, at the same time, be entertained by some good stories. And if it was the right time of year, leave the shop with a big bag full of fresh tomatoes, cucumbers, and corn from his garden, probably amounting to a value of two or three dollars. First Choice Hairstylists would be hard pressed to match that value.

Duncan also taught me how to adapt to working for Jack McRae. "Don't be afraid of him. All he can do is fire you. But whatever you do, don't feed him any bullshit," he said. "He will catch you, sure as shootin'. He is a regular human polygraph machine." Once again he was right. Mr. McRae constantly asked questions. He would ask the same question in different ways, at different times, probably remembering the first answer. "How much yellow birch veneer can we expect to cut this winter in that area east of Dividing Lake?" he would ask me. And I would provide my estimate, "A hundred and fifty thousand board feet." In a week or so, he would ask, "How much veneer is in that area south of Whatnot Lakes—thirty or forty thousand feet?" It would be the same area, and I had to be sure to provide the same answer. It wasn't always easy.

Three or four years before I arrived at Rock Lake, McRae's had purchased two Blue-Ox skidders. These were the first wheeled skidders (large four-wheel-drive machines used to pull logs from the stump to the roadside) to be manufactured. They had a fixed frame with direct steering, and were much like a truck equipped with a winch. Operators would often break their thumbs as the steering wheel whipped around when a front wheel struck a stump or a rock. Mechanics couldn't replace broken axles fast enough.

They were an operational disaster and were soon decommissioned, relegated to plowing snow. "If it can't eat hay, it's no damned good for skidding logs," the boss shouted. "I don't want to see anymore of those goddamned wheeled skidders around this place, ever."

In the meantime, the manufacturers were working hard to improve the skidders. They finally developed a sturdier articulating-frame design, which made the machine more manoeuvrable and efficient and became the prototype of the modern-day skidder.

One day, a Timberjack Co. sales representative showed up at the Rock Lake mill. He knew enough not to drop into the Airy office for fear that he would end up at the bottom of Galeairy Lake. He offered a demonstration skidder to Donald for a couple of weeks, at no charge. Donald agreed and it was shipped to us the next day. There wasn't a stampede to share the news of this development with "the boss."

Gary Cannon was the operator, and I was with him for a few days conducting time studies and recording productivity and costs. It performed extremely well and out-produced the small skidding tractors and horses dramatically. It didn't take long for the news to spread. The camp buzzed with the prospects of wholesale changes coming up. One afternoon, Mr. McRae arrived at the mill and, over supper, heard the men talking about the skidder.

It didn't take him long to confront us in the office after supper that night. He was ready to do battle! The group consisted of Duncan, foreman Paul Kuiack, clerk Paddy Roche, and myself. Donald was the lucky one. He was at home in Whitney.

"Holy old whistlin' Jesus," he screamed. "You bastards are going to drive me out of business. I have a good notion to fire the whole damned bunch of you tonight. It's a son-of-a-bitch of a terror anyway." He stomped around the room and kicked over a small stool.

I was shocked. I had not witnessed an outburst like this in my whole life. The others were more experienced. At one point, I looked over at Dunc, who was sitting calmly in his chair, barely visible behind a cloud of smoke. I was trying to catch his eye to plead, "My God, Dunc, you have to help us out here."

I wasn't disappointed. After a few minutes, he got out of his chair and walked over to the window that looked out over the mill. "The boss" had stopped for a breather and to hitch his pants up. Dunc motioned towards the mill and said quietly, "You know yourself, Jack. You have one of the most modern and best-equipped hardwood sawmills in Eastern Canada, and I don't see any goddamned horses hauling the lumber out to the yard or feeding the mill with logs. No, sir. Instead, you have four shiny-new, rubber-tired, front-end loaders to do that—state-of-the-art for sure! And you want these boys to make you money in the bush by using some damn tired old nags that should have gone to the glue factory years ago. It's a wonder you don't have them skidding logs with oxen. You are going to have to give them a chance to explore new methods and equipment—then they will make some money for you. Loosen up on the reins or you will choke these thoroughbreds."

Right away, Mr. McRae recognized the validity of Dunc's message. He sat down in a chair and mellowed completely—and without a whimper. I couldn't believe it. I felt like cheering. A few minutes later they were all laughing and joking about days gone by at Hay Lake.

I shook my head in amazement. Another lesson learned. Soft words, backed up by reasoned and organized thoughts. And the lion tamer had performed his magic. Wow!

However, I could also see the merit of Dunc's previous advice: "Don't bullshit him or he will catch up to you." And I guess that is what we did by keeping him in the dark—never again!

Alcohol was not openly consumed at Rock Lake, although it's expected that it was not far off-site. The closest thing to drinking on the job was Frank Shalla adding a thimble full of brandy to a fresh can of snuff. A pinch of that would lift you into the treetops.

Paddy Roche was known to be occasionally overdue on trips to Huntsville when picking up parcels at the bus station for the mill. Dunc once remarked that "the first thing Paddy does when he arrives in Huntsville is to check at the beer store—in case the bus driver dropped the parcel off there by mistake." Duncan also liked his beer, especially in the summer, when he was out in his boat fishing on Whitefish Lake. He always had an ample supply stashed under lumber piles and behind the drying shed—like a squirrel.

One day, I was working in the office and Andrew Sydock stopped to pick up a load ticket on his way to the planing mill in Bancroft with a load of lumber. We chatted for a few minutes before he left. He was barely out of sight when I spotted Dunc sprinting across the yard towards the office. "Has Andrew left yet?" he asked breathlessly. "He left a minute ago, Dunc," I replied.

"Son-of-bitch, I hid my weekend case of beer in a lift of lumber that he has on his truck. Can you call the planing mill and ask them to return it? It will be just like those bastards in Bancroft to drink it on me." I called and it was back at Rock Lake before supper.

I met up with Andrew in 1999. He was on a nostalgia tour that Bill Hubbert and I conducted for some of the older retired men I had worked with during my McRae days (more on that amazing day later). I hadn't seen Andrew for thirty-four years and asked him if he remembered the incident. "Sure do," he said, "and I think that it was me who had brought the case of beer from Bancroft to Duncan in the first place. It wasn't the first or the last one that got away on him."

Duncan was invaluable to McRae Lumber Company and worked for them until the age of seventy-three. His career ended when he was seriously injured by a moving truck in the Whitney mill yard. In addition to performing his regular work as a lumber grader and yard supervisor, he was constantly on the watch for opportunities to improve the overall operations of the company—and the well-being of his co-workers, who all had such great affection for him. J.S.L., Donald and, in later years, John and Bob, relied heavily on him for that.

One example that comes to mind during my time at Rock Lake was the Ted Kuiack story. Teddy had worked for McRae for many years and was the stationary engineer in the mill's boiler room. When the mill was operating, he worked seven days a week and knew the boiler and steam system inside and out. Unfortunately with changing regulations, the Department of Labour was insisting that his official certification be upgraded to the next level. He had tried writing the examination a couple of times, without success. He found the process intimidating, and with his limited education had difficulty expressing himself in writing.

The officials were beginning to press McRae. A couple of deadlines had been missed, and the issue was heating up. Teddy was one of the highest paid men in the mill, but this could mean him losing his job and being assigned to another, lesser-paying one in the mill. It also meant that McRae would have to bring a replacement in from the outside, at increased cost and risk.

It was Dunc who suggested to "the boss" that he call the department and see if they would agree to have me act as Teddy's scribe at the examination. They agreed, with the condition that we come to Toronto to write the exam under close supervision. I was to ask Teddy the questions and record his answers, without discussion. It was apparent that I would need to familiarize myself with the technology and the terminology, as I had no previous knowledge or experience with the subject.

During the next six weeks I was with Teddy every spare minute that I had. (I flashed back to the day of my interview when Mr. McRae said, "There won't be enough to keep a forester busy, but we'll find other things for you to do.") He taught me as much as I was capable of learning about steam and refrigeration. There were manuals for me to read at home, and Teddy tested me on what he had showed me in previous sessions. I was seeing valves and gauges in my sleep. He was an excellent teacher, and I'm sure I am the only forester in Canada to have had such intensive training in the operation of a wood-fired boiler.

Finally the day arrived, and Teddy and I drove to Toronto in Donald's brand-new Buick. That night we treated ourselves to a big steak at the Royal York. As we strolled along Yonge Street taking in the sights, we remarked that it is was a far different scene than could be seen out the front window of Greg's Shell on a snowy Tuesday night in February.

Teddy was up at 4:30 the next morning ready to get at it. But this gave him too much time to worry about the upcoming morning. He was a basket case by the time we sat down to start at 8:30 a.m. However, his anxiety was short-lived. Within minutes his answers flowed freely. It was difficult to slow him down enough to be able to record the answers properly. He was operating on a "full head of steam," so to speak, providing five-minute answers when a one-minute answer would have sufficed. It was a gruelling four-hour exam, and when we finished we both knew that he had done well.

We were so excited and busy reviewing the exam that while driving home on the 401, I missed the exit at Peterborough. We drove a hundred miles out of our way. I chewed Copenhagen snuff in those days, and can recall Donald growling his displeasure the next day when he saw the tobacco streaks down the side of his shiny new car.

Teddy called me one night a few weeks later to tell me he had received his certificate in the mail that day. I went down to his home, and we sat at his kitchen table sipping on a glass of rum and Coke and gazing at the certificate, cherishing the moment.

Teddy and I were able to reflect on this experience many years after I left Whitney. I had a nice visit with him, when he and his wife provided a room in their home for our daughter, Christine, who had a summer job in a resort on Galeairy Lake.

There were many sides to Duncan MacGregor and one of the most enjoyable was his love of the practical joke. I was his target on at least one occasion. Dunc found out somehow that I had a weak stomach and would tease me about it. Especially at meal time. If someone were to fart in the next township, I would be out the door in a flash, throwing up in the snowbank.

For a while, Tommy Cannon had been beset by a bad case of piles. He was commonly seen scratching his ass when the need arose. It reminded me of the drive camp on the Baskatong. (I suggest that the only time a cook should scratch his ass is after the cookery is shut down for the day and the lights are out.)

We were having breakfast in the Rock Lake cookery one morning. Duncan and I were sitting across from each other at the end of the table closest to the kitchen, where Tommy was working. I was munching on a piece of toast, waiting for the cookee to bring a platter of hot eggs.

Dunc glanced towards the kitchen and, with a twinkle in his eye, nodded for me to have a look. He said, "Brent, your eggs are coming right up."

I looked over and there was Tommy, flipping eggs with his right hand, his left arm up his ass to the elbow. My gagging was rendered mute by Dunc's outburst of wheezy laughter. But I was hungry and didn't leave the table, quite content to have pickled herring on toast for my breakfast that morning.

Earlier I mentioned about how Duncan did me in on the morning that I was chasing margarine orders for Mr. McRae. It was an ugly morning. Everything was ice-covered, nothing was moving. It was around 7 a.m. I had picked up my half-ton at the garage and had a couple of helpers with me. We were going to sand roads for the trucks. Unfortunately, we had no sand on board—the sand pit was a couple of miles from the millsite. I had to gas up first, so I came down the hill past the cookery to the office at the bottom of the hill, where the pump was.

I filled up with gas, but on the first try the truck couldn't make it up the hill to the cookery. I backed up and tried it again, and again, and again, each time only gaining about five feet.

By this time, the gallery had assembled. I could see Dunc, Paddy and Henry Corcoran, a log buyer from Canada Veneers in Pembroke, who was spending the winter with us. They were looking out the window and, on each failed attempt, I could see them laughing and clapping. They were being well entertained as I hung on to the wheel like a NASCAR driver, while my truck spun around like a top.

My patience was wearing thin. I decided to back up behind the mill as far as I could go, expecting that, from that distance, there would be enough momentum to make it to the top. My helpers stood on the back bumper for additional weight. I took off like a scalded dog around the end of the mill, my chums with their heads down and holding onto the tailgate for dear life, the end of the truck swinging wildly, almost out of control.

I knew that I was going to make it this time. The audience in the office could find something else to laugh at. As I approached the office, Henry came running out of the office door, frantically waving a piece of paper. Like a damned idiot, I pulled up and stopped halfway up the hill, expecting that it was an important message from Donald or Mr. McRae.

With a huge grin on his face, Henry passed me the paper through the truck window. It was a message from Dunc: "If you make it up to the cookery by noon, I'll meet you there for a cup of tea."

That old bugger! I was ready to choke him. I jumped out of my truck and stormed into the office. There he was, his face beet red, wheezing himself silly from laughing—and pounding his knees with his hands. What could I do but join in on the laughter and fun! But I told him, "I'll get you sometime, you old son-of-bitch; you better keep your head up." But I never did! We made it up the hill on the next try amidst a hail of cheers.

It was with a huge lump in my throat that I said goodbye to Dunc in 1965 when I left Rock Lake. He was very special to me. I saw him a couple of times at the mill in the mid seventies, when I began working for the AFA, and visited him once in the Huntsville hospital after his accident. In typical fashion, he was charming the nurses and almost had them convinced to let him have his tobacco, but not quite. They all loved him.

When I first met Dunc again after all those years, he said to me, "Holy old bald-headed Nellie, Brent, I can't believe that you are working for the goddamned government now. Have you lost your mind? How do you expect a government outfit to look after logging in Algonquin Park? The mills will run out of logs and we will all starve—sure as shootin'." He wasn't the only one who doubted that it could be pulled off. It sure would have been nice to be able to give him the full report on the success of the AFA after twenty-five years. He would have been impressed.

A few years ago Heather and I drove to P.E.I. for a holiday. We took "two full weeks" to make the trip—"by the holy old whistlin'." A few days before leaving, I was into the McRae office in Whitney to visit John and Bob on business. We reminisced about Dunc, and Bob pulled out a box of audio tapes made of Duncan, Donald, Frank Shalla and others, as they sat around talking at a kitchen table over a pot of tea.

I borrowed some of the tapes and played them during our trip. It was a wonderful way to relive our relationship. Yes, Duncan MacGregor may not have travelled much in his lifetime, but one summer, he came along with Heather and me on a trip to P.E.I. It was with sadness that I was unable to attend his funeral in Huntsville. I was out of town on business at the time.

In July 2004, Heather and I stayed for a few days at the Mew Lake campsite in Algonquin Park. One bright sunny morning, we biked down the old railroad right-of-way to the former Rock Lake mill site. It was a beautiful ride and is highly recommended to all park visitors. We sang gleefully, as we pedalled along the peaceful shorelines of the Lake of Two Rivers and Whitefish Lake, through a dense canopy of huge, over-mature yellow birch and maple trees. After checking us out with a quick look and the nod of his head, a young bear crossed the path ahead of us.

All the structures at the mill site had been removed, the site rehabilitated and planted with red pine trees. But in my mind everything was still there—just as I had left it.

Heather took a picture of me on my bike at the same spot on the hill where I had stopped my truck forty years before to pick up Duncan's message. I could see him peering out the window, waving and laughing his fool head off. "Yes sireee, Dunc. I'm back, if only on two wheels this time. I am going to try and drive up that hill one more time just for you." And I did!

> *"Any man who would boil tea water over a softwood fire would be fool enough to put on a pair of mitts to bait a fishhook."*
>
> —"Hay Lake" Joe Lavalley, native guide and trapper

One summer I had to conduct some extensive timber cruising in preparation for a twenty-year forest management plan for submission to the Ontario Department of Lands and Forests. The plan was a prerequisite to the issuance of approval to harvest Crown timber. Timber cruising is an "on-the-ground inventory sampling process." Plots are established along a cruise line within a systematic grid, and standing trees are measured to determine timber volume by tree quality, age, site class, and species. Sample plot data is then extended to determine the volume of timber in localized forest stands and eventually the whole forest.

A three-man crew was required: a compassman, who walked two chains (132 feet) ahead of the other two crew members to set the direction of the line; a cruiser to assess the trees and measure their diameters with calipers; and a tallyman to record the data.

I needed a couple of good physically fit men who wouldn't get lost in the bush and were capable of walking all day over rough terrain. We could not deviate from the location of pre-set compass lines, thus it was necessary to traverse difficult features such as swamps, rocky side hills, and windfallen trees. Not all loggers could fit the bill. I have known more than one pot-bellied bulldozer operator who could scarcely make it from the seat of his dozer to the seat of his half-ton.

Bush orientation skills were important. One cutter I worked with in Lake Superior Park left his chainsaw on a stump to come down to the log landing to have lunch with the rest of the crew. Later, somebody had to go looking for him. He was lost for the afternoon trying to find his saw.

Mr. McRae and Duncan MacGregor matched me up with two of the best: "Hay Lake" Joe Lavalley and Eddie Coghlan. Joe was a good friend of Dunc's, and both he and Eddie had worked for McRae off and on over the years. They were free spirits, preferring the more unregulated and unrestricted life of trapping and guiding, with a little farming and woodcutting on the side.

Eddie was a quiet man who usually sported a month-long growth of whiskers showing traces of cigarette tobacco, dead blackflies, and other debris. He would walk all day through the bush, hardly saying a word.

He told us over our lunch fire one day, as he was chewing on a chunk of steak from supper the night before, that during the previous winter he had lost a couple of lower teeth and found it difficult to chew. "I was having a hell of a time eating," he said. "So I filed down a couple of teeth from a beaver that I had trapped and wired them to another good tooth. Works real good and a lot cheaper than hitchhiking to Barry's Bay to get screwed by a son-of-a-bitch of a dentist."

Eddie didn't smile much, so I don't know if I ever saw those beaver teeth, but it wasn't for the lack of trying to make him laugh.

I was telling a good friend of mine, Kenny Purcell from L'Original, Ontario, about Eddie's tooth transplant. The subject led to a discussion about the advances in dentistry over the years, from the old slow-moving mechanical pulley and belt drills, to the modern high-speed electric and air drills.

Kenny knew a fellow years ago with a face-wide, "curls-on-the-end," military handlebar moustache. Once he was in the dentist's chair, and when he leaned over to spit into the cup, caught his "pride and joy" moustache in the moving belt of the drill. The dentist had to cut the belt to relieve the howling patient!

On the other hand, "Hay Lake" Joe, a Métis, was always smiling and could talk the wheel off a log truck. He was a slim wiry man, in excellent shape from a lifetime of physical activity—a striking figure with his distinctive Roman nose and pitch black hair. He lived on his small farm in Sabine Township near Hay Lake.

There were, or had been, at least three Joe Lavalleys in the Whitney and Hay Lake areas. "Yes, sir," Joe claimed, "to make sure there wouldn't be a mix-up, they named me 'Hay Lake Joe.' I was born in the bow of a birchbark canoe on Hay Lake, while my father paddled like hell for the shore for help. And that's no bullshit."

Joe was like a cat in the bush. He walked without making a sound and could be four feet directly behind without me knowing he was there. It was eerie! He always had his nose slightly elevated, sniffing like a bloodhound, and occasionally telling us if there was a beaver house over the hill out of sight. And sure enough, we would walk over the hill and there it was. He never missed.

He was constantly stopping to check on animal tracks, or sticking his head into the cavity of a tree, or crawling around on his hands and knees under an overturned stump to see what animal was living there. His repertoire of bird calls could rival any sophisticated modern-day birder. Birds followed us all day, and the whisky-jacks would be well treated at lunchtime.

Lunch was an important time for Joe and Eddie. They would start collecting birchbark and looking for the right site a half hour before we stopped. We had to have good water, dry hardwood for the fire, and dry seats. If there were no dry seats, some would be made out of birchbark.

On our first day out Joe told me, "Any man who would boil his tea water over a softwood fire should be made to spend a week snuggled up to a bear hibernating in his den." Watching Joe make tea was something to behold. It was necessary to have loose tea leaves, of course. "Any man who would use tea bags should be thrown into the bear's den with that 'other fella.'"

Once the water started to boil in the tea pail, Joe removed the pail and put it down away from the fire for a few seconds. He put it back over the fire until it boiled again, and then removed it again. He did this four times—not three times or five times. It had to be four times. After the fourth time, he set the pail down and added a handful of cold water to settle the leaves to the bottom. Best tea known to man!

Joe could do anything with birchbark. One day, I forgot to pack a teacup in my lunch bag, so he took a huge hunting knife out of its holster, cut a piece of bark, and shaped it into a cone-like vessel. Then, he cut a small crooked stick, and with a split cut in one end, slid the stick over the joint of the cone. The split stick served as a handle as it held the cone together, like a clothes pin. It resembled a small ladle.

He claimed, while holding back a slight grin, that he could boil water in it—if the bark had come from a birch tree growing on a northeast slope and was soaked in water for seven-and-one-half days. He didn't demonstrate, so I remain sceptical on that one.

On one other very cold and miserable day in May, we could see a heavy rain storm coming up. Joe went to a large white birch tree with his knife and, within minutes, had crafted a shawl-like cover with a cut-out neck to keep our shoulders dry. Not something you would come across on the racks of a Mark's Work Wearhouse store.

When foresters get together, in a spirit of brotherhood, they will share their experiences, termed in the business as "play-with-pay" days. Something like doctors and lawyers playing golf on Wednesday afternoons, but not nearly as regular or frequent. These activities have absolutely nothing to do with the work, but are not a holiday. Reference to the phenomenon will never be found in the Ontario Professional Foresters Association's Code of Ethics.

"Hay Lake" Joe, Eddie, and I had one such day. This is probably only the second or third time that I have ever told the story and, as I do, I hesitate—with a vision of "the boss" lacing up his shiny black boots to get ready to come and find me.

It was an excruciatingly hot day in early July. It began normally, except that we left camp earlier than usual that morning to beat the heat. We drove our truck to the outlet of Lake Louisa and canoed up the lake to a point where the cruise line or sample area was to start. There was not even the hint of a breeze. The lake was still, resembling a huge mirror, with the final traces of a morning mist dancing on the water and a far-off loon yodelling our arrival.

I could recall having difficulty laying out the line on a map when looking at the aerial photographs in the office, as there was a steep hemlock rock bluff running for some distance along the shoreline. It wasn't possible to offset the line. And as we needed sample plots in the area, there was no choice but to climb the rock face. We were like three mountain goats, crawling up to the top, which was about 150 feet above lake level. When we finally arrived, completely exhausted, we stopped for a smoke and to marvel at our accomplishment and the scene below. Joe pulled out his pipe and lit up a bowlful of Old Chum.

The birds were singing, and there we were, looking out over one of the most beautiful lakes in Algonquin Park. It didn't get much better than that!

And then the day took an unplanned turn. Old Joe, with his incessant curiosity and adventurous spirit, spotted a huge stone teetering on the edge of the cliff. It had been placed there ten thousand years ago by a receding glacier and was just waiting for three boneheaded timber cruisers to come along and simply blow it into Lake Louisa.

The stone was about the size of two normal upright refrigerators. It had an angular base, which sat precariously on another flat stone. Joe went over to the stone and put his shoulder to it, and it moved. "You know, I think we can roll that son-of-a-bitch right down into the lake. Wouldn't that be something to see?" he remarked, wringing his hands in glee, like a little boy at the top of a hill with a new toboggan.

Eddie and I joined him and we all pushed together. It moved some more, but not enough to go over the edge. Before there was any further discussion about what to do next, Joe was swinging his axe to cut a six-inch maple for use as a lever. This was going to do it. No, it didn't, but close. Next came another lever and another. Now we each had one—making progress for sure!

We worked like dogs in blistering heat for over two hours before it went over. When it did, it only went down about fifty feet to snuggle up against a big yellow birch tree. It didn't make it to the lake. The mission had failed!

We had cleared a quarter acre of trees on the top of the hill and, with tongues hanging out from exhaustion, hadn't done a lick of work for McRae yet. "Holy old whistlin'."

At that point, I did what I should have done three hours before. As crew boss, I took charge of the situation. We walked back down the hill to the lake and dove in the lake for a soothing swim. A pot of tea was boiled as we enjoyed our "working-man's lunch." It had been a tiring morning, so we rested for a few minutes after lunch, then jumped into the canoe and paddled and fished our way across the lake. An easy short cruise line was completed to finish up the day. We paid the price the next day, however. The heat wave was still with us, and we had to work from dawn to dusk to catch up. It was worth it for me, though. It is one of the best memories I have of Algonquin Park.

Some day, I am going to return to Lake Louisa to find that stone. If the tree is still there, the stone will be. I know I could find it. Maybe some of my grandchildren will accompany me, and we will coax that old stone the rest of the way into the lake. At that point, we will boil some tea over a hardwood fire and I will make a toast: "Thanks for the memory, my good friends, 'Hay Lake' Joe and Eddie."

A couple of weeks later, we were timber-cruising in Clyde Township and were late leaving the bush one night, probably still making up for the "playday." I was driving, and we were on a Hydro line road, which was prohibited to public travel. Not expecting to meet anyone, and probably driving a little too fast, we came around a sharp corner and met a one-ton truck coming in the opposite direction.

We met with a glancing front-end collision, and our truck flipped over on its side into the ditch. There were no seat belts in those days, and Eddie was thrown from the vehicle. He was jolted, but not seriously injured. Joe, who was sitting in the middle, was unscathed. Luckily, I was wearing my hard hat, and my head hit the wrap-around windshield frame, causing a laceration on my forehead, otherwise I was OK. The other vehicle was travelling to a youth camp in Haliburton. It was carrying a half dozen teenaged boys, who were standing up in the back hanging onto the staked sides of the truck. They were fortunately uninjured, with the exception of one boy who had a slight cut on his knee.

We were not equipped with radios and had no way to seek help. It was a miracle that no one was seriously injured. Our truck was damaged beyond repair, and a few days later, Mr. McRae commented to me, "Damn good thing that you wrecked that truck and not a newer one—it was costing too much and we were going to replace it anyway." It was decided that Joe, Eddie, and I walk the ten miles to Whitney and the other group would remain at the scene, in case someone came along. We arrived in Whitney shortly after nine. I called the OPP, Donald, and others on behalf of the youth camp, took a couple of aspirins, and went to bed.

Around eleven o'clock the phone rang. It was Dr. Post, Whitney's only doctor. News travelled fast in Whitney, and he was calling to find out how I was. "You will need to get down to my office right away for a tetanus shot," he ordered. That was typical of Doc Post, a most dedicated and beloved doctor in his community.

Dr. Gilbert (Gib) Post had been a skilled big-city surgeon who, for health reasons, returned to his home town as a general practitioner. He presided over a three-room "Red Cross Hospital" in town. To this day, Dr. Post remains a legend in Whitney, where he is remembered with great affection by residents, many of whom were delivered by this gentle man.

Dunc told me once that Dr. Post had his own form of medicare, which often left him on the short end. He collected one dollar a month as a payroll deduction from employees of companies such as

McRae's. This entitled the person and his family to have access to his care, which would frequently be in their homes. When it was necessary for a patient to attend another hospital for major surgery, in a larger centre such as Peterborough, Dr. Post's medicare fund underwrote the cost, if not in whole at least in part, depending on the circumstances.

My own personal experience with Doc Post included his delivery of our son John. It was a bright sunny Saturday afternoon in October. He didn't want me inside the hospital to get in his way. I was assigned outside to the car to listen to a "Big Four" football game between the Alouettes and Argonauts. In about an hour, he came out still dressed in his hospital garments and sat down to listen to the game for a few minutes. Finally, he said, "By the way, you have a kicking little linebacker in there. Do you want to see him?"

Sandy MacGregor, a cousin of Duncan's, was McRae's "walking boss" and had worked for him for more than thirty years. (A walking boss travelled through logging areas in advance of logging operations to locate and build main haul roads and camps.) The job, naturally, required a lot of walking, and since Sandy was in his mid sixties, he was beginning to slow down. He was unable to continue doing the job and eventually retired.

He took a less physically demanding job with the Werlick Company, which manufactured wooden toys. It operated a sawmill and logging operation north of Huntsville, where Sandy lived. One day, as he was driving into the bush, he encountered a couple of timber wolves standing in the middle of the road. They had been feeding on a deer carcass nearby.

Sandy stopped and got out of his truck, shouted, and threw stones at the animals. They turned and attacked Sandy, his yells attracting other loggers, who were working close by. When they arrived, the wolves retreated. Sandy was taken to the hospital where he remained a couple of days for observation and received treatment for lacerations. I have encountered wolves many times in the park, especially while at Rock Lake, but this was the only instance I am aware of that resulted in a person being attacked.

Paddy Roche and his brother Phil were two other favourites of mine. Paddy was a quiet snow-white-haired Irishman from the hills of Wilno, who worked as the clerk at Rock Lake. He was also the company scaler, measuring log production in the bush as basis for paying loggers, who were working on piecework. He looked after payroll and also presided over "camp orders." Employees were paid monthly, and if one was a little short during the month, he visited Paddy. A camp order would be made requesting an advance on his wages. Camp orders were closely monitored by "the boss," giving him the opportunity to keep an eye on some of the younger men, who would have their monthly wages drawn by the end of the second week.

Phil had worked for McRae for many years and had left before my arrival. He operated a real estate and insurance business in Whitney, and he nominated former MPP Sean Conway as Liberal candidate in Renfrew County when Sean first ran in 1975. Phil was one of the best storytellers ever to sit around a kitchen table. His eloquent, soft-spoken descriptions and timely delivery of the punchline were a work of art.

Phil once told me about visiting an old fellow, who had a small house on the outskirts of Madawaska. They were sitting in the kitchen, and Phil had to deliver the bad news that his fire insurance premium was to increase by a significant amount that year.

"What in hell is the reason for that, Phil?" the old fellow asked.

"Well, Henry," Phil replied, "it's because you live in an unprotected area without ready access to water."

The old fellow grumbled for a minute or two and then said to Phil as he walked over to a door leading into the basement, "Come here and have a look."

He opened the door and Phil looked down to see water within two feet from the top of the stairs. "Is that enough goddamned water for you, Phil?" he snapped.

Paul Kuiack was McRae's bush foreman. He and I travelled together frequently, locating logging areas and roads in advance of the cutting and skidding operations. Paul lived in Wilno and had a following of Polish loggers from that community who worked for McRae's.

One winter, Paul needed some extra logging crews in the camp. Jack McRae sent him down to the Wilno Tavern one evening to see if he could hire some good men. Paul asked me to come along for the experience and, as I was to discover later on, to help with the driving.

Draft beer was ten cents a glass, and Mr. McRae gave us $15 to treat the boys. He added, "If you don't need to spend it all, bring back the goddamned change." We were like the old-time ranch foremen visiting the Old West saloon to hire cowboys for the cattle drive. That little tavern in Wilno rollicked that night. There was no change to return, but Paul lined up a few men, who reported to work at Rock Lake the following week. Mission accomplished!

One fall day, Paul and I were walking along the park boundary in the vicinity of Hollow Creek. The area is in the southwestern section of the park and only accessible by old logging roads from the Dorset area. At that time, the park boundary was not cut out as it is today. As a result, we mistakenly crossed over the line and were walking down a large hill trying to find old boundary markings or tree blazes. Upon arrival at the bottom of the hill, we sighted something unusual hidden behind by a thick cover of small spruce and balsam trees.

We went over to investigate and found a small log cabin. It was in excellent condition. The short, low-hanging door was closed, but unlocked, and inside was a cedarstrip canoe, numerous beaver traps, and a sleeping bag spread out on the single bunk. Clothing items were scattered around, a few utensils and tin dishes sat on the table beside dried-up jars of mustard and jam. Evidence of mice and squirrels was everywhere. A calendar on the wall was outdated by two or three years. It was apparent that there hadn't been anyone there for some time.

We were very puzzled with our discovery. Even though the cabin appeared to be abandoned, there still was a good canoe and traps inside. We wondered, "Why had the trapper not returned?"

Our findings were reported to the Department of Lands and Forests in Whitney, and we didn't hear anything for several months. Finally, a conservation officer told us they had discovered that, a couple of winters before, a trapper from the village of Dorset had become ill in the bush. He was barely able to make it home and died a couple of weeks later. This may have been the same trapper.

As I reflect on that scene, it appeared that although he may have left prematurely, he was strong enough to carry his canoe inside. It is my hope that his family or friends were eventually able to find that little cabin to salvage the canoe, and to be able to sense the feeling that the bushman would have had to be sick in such a remote location, so far from medical assistance and the comfort of family.

Paul and I, also unexpectedly, came across the remains of an old "camboose" camp one day. A camboose camp was used to accommodate loggers in the mid to late 1880s. It was a one-room, low-profile log structure, which served as sleeping quarters with two men sleeping beside each other on double-tiered bunks. An open hearth in middle of the building was the only source of heat and was also used by the cook to prepare meals. A tapered hole in the roof took away the smoke and the smell of stinking socks. The men slept, ate, dried their clothes, and told stories after supper around the fire in the hearth, which burned around the clock.

We spent an hour trying to figure out where each component of the camp was located (for example, the horse stable, blacksmith shop, and living area). It is difficult to describe the thrill of finding an old camp, which probably had not had any visitors since the last loggers left more than a century before. We were like little boys finding a chest of gold.

I have explored many old camps such as these. When coming across the remains, the camp garbage pits were sought out first, the ones nearest the blacksmith shops being the most revealing. It was there that wonderful old treasures could be found: coloured bottles, discarded boots, broken tools, sleigh and wagon parts. They were hidden museums, showcasing the lives of rugged men from another era.

In 2001, Ontario Parks, with financial assistance from the AFA, established the Big Pine Trail. The parking lot to access the hiking trail is on Highway 60 directly across from the Rock Lake Road. The Big Pine Trail features magnificent old-growth pine trees, and at the end of the trail, next to a small

pond, are the remains of an old pine logging camp that was active around 1900. Its location was unknown, until Jack Mihell, a logging history hobbyist and forester, formerly employed by the Ministry of Natural Resources and Ontario Parks, discovered it nearly a century later.
The visitor can see the outline of the stable, bunkhouse, cookery, and blacksmith shop—and imagine what it was like to live and work there. It is highly recommended for anyone with an interest in logging history. A state-of-the-art logging museum is situated a few miles down the road towards Whitney, if you want to make a day out of it.

If there ever was a one-man band, it was Gary Cannon. A big, hard-working and outgoing logger, his trademark was a booming laugh and friendly greeting. He was Tommy Cannon's nephew and, in later years, became McRae's logging superintendent. He could operate anything mechanical that was controlled by levers or a steering wheel.

When I first met him he was a pieceworker skidding logs in the bush with a small tractor. Before going to the bush in the morning to do his regular job, he would check at the garage to see if there was a log truck not scheduled to work that day. If there was one available, he would drive it to the bush instead of driving in the crew bus. At night, after a hard day's work, he brought a load of logs out to the mill.

One spring, when the roads were wet, Gary worked for a few days as a one-man road maintenance crew, repairing soft spots in the road. He had a tandem gravel truck, a grader, and a front-end loader located in a gravel pit. He was the lone operator. I was driving out of the bush one night and, from the top of a big hill west of Lake Louisa, witnessed one of the most unbelievable and dexterous exhibitions of man and machine imaginable.

It all happened so fast I couldn't get there quickly enough to help him. I just sat there in my truck and stared in amazement. Gary had his dump truck stuck to the axles in a mud hole. He had the front of the truck chained to the rear of the grader to try to pull it out. Next, he started the truck, put it in gear, until the wheels began to spin. Then, he propped the accelerator down with an axe and ran like a rabbit to the grader, which pulled the truck out of the mud, and then backed the grader into the truck to stall it, so it would not run away or break something. There should be a hall of fame somewhere for a man like that.

As I think about Gary Cannon and his work ethic, I amuse myself speculating about how he would react to being approached by a union organizer to form a union at McRae's. The term that comes to mind is "airborne."

I am also reminded of another amusing incident involving Gary. In the mid 1990s, Ontario Parks officials were having difficulty controlling public access on various roads into the park. To fix the problem, they undertook an extensive program of installing gates on these roads.

Gary used one such road to move logging equipment to and from his operations. He had heard that a gate had been erected, but had not yet received a key, so he stopped in at the park headquarters one day and met his old chum Jack Borrowman, who was a supervisor with Ontario Parks. Gary posed the question, "Will you be giving me a key for the lock on that gate, Jack, or should I bring my axe?" Alas, things were about to change! Whitney had been good to me, and I liked living there and working in Algonquin Park. The McRae family had been very kind to my family and me—McRae Lumber Co. had been an excellent employer. However, the company was a small family-owned operation, and the opportunity for my advancement was minimal. The only time I was able to interact with other forester colleagues was on a occasional trip to the Department of Lands and Forests office in Pembroke. I also couldn't shake the memory of Mansiel Wilson; it was time to get the job-search antennae out of the attic.

Copies of the trade magazine *The Canadian Forest Industries* were always available at the Rock Lake office for employees to read. I would bring old copies home, as our four-year-old son Brent would like to jump up on my knee and look at pictures of trucks and bulldozers.

In a twist of fate one day, he retrieved a copy of the magazine from a box in the back shed. As we leafed through it again, there it was—a small ad on the last page: "Weyerhaeuser Canada Ltd. requires a graduate forester to locate haul roads on their logging operations north of Sault Ste. Marie." And that was to be the beginning of the next adventure.

When Heather and I drove to P.E.I. with Duncan MacGregor, Don McRae, and half of Whitney coming along with us on audio tape, we made an amazing discovery. It was fascinating to learn of the pride that some old-time Islanders have in being able to boast that, in their lifetime, they have never been off the island. To them, mainland Nova Scotia and New Brunswick is foreign ground, commonly referred to as "the other side."

Well-known P.E.I. historian and storyteller David Weale described the response he received once when he asked an old-time Islander, "Have you ever been to the 'the other side'?"

"No, I'm pleased to say," replied the old timer with a grin, "but I slept with a woman from Halifax one time."

To the old timers of Whitney, "the other side" may have been Toronto, Ottawa, Montreal, or even Prince Edward Island. There would be no need leave Whitney; everything was at the fingertips!

Doc Post, his medicare system, and the three-room hospital were available to everybody—the Peterborough hospital was just over two hours away.

McRae Lumber Co. looked after its employees, was on solid footing, and the next generation of family members was on the horizon. There was hunting and fishing on the doorstep, hockey on the outdoor community rink in the winter, swimming in the crystal-clear waters of the public beach on Galerairy Lake, and bowling in Bancroft on Friday nights.

The bootlegger, who lived within walking distance of all residents, charged only for the cost of his product, plus gas to Barry's Bay and back. His profit was the enjoyment of visitors arriving on his doorstep in the wee hours and staying a while to share a few stories.

Rabbit ears would pick up one snowy television channel. A twenty-foot aerial on the chimney would get you two more snowy channels.

The big Catholic church on the hill was constantly alive with bake sales, bazaars, masses, and dances. And the priest who, like Doc Post, was on call twenty-four hours a day, knew everyone by their first names.

A housewife could be rolling bread dough on her kitchen counter and glance out the window to wave at her mother or sister doing the same thing across the road. Brothers and neighbours pooled their half-tons and chainsaws to cut, haul, and split firewood for their winter supply.

Friends visited each other regularly, gathered and laughed around kitchen tables drinking gallons of tea and snacking on Polish sausage and homemade biscuits. Occasionally on a Saturday night, a bottle of Captain Morgan rum would be fetched from the pantry.

They leaned on and cared for each other. Life was good in Whitney.

The only ones who needed to go to "the other side" were youngsters heading off to university or college, or to work in the bright lights—and people like me, who had come from "the other side" in the first place. So, it was a bright spring day in 1965 when I said my farewells to Dunc, Donald, "the boss," and others, as I left for Sault Ste. Marie and the Highlands of Algoma.

Chapter 3—This, That, And The Other Thing

"Cowboys ride horses ... loggers drive pickup trucks."

—Brent Connelly, forester

If you drive through Whitney, Barry's Bay, Mattawa, Huntsville, or Pembroke any day of the week before 6 a.m., you will see them: black or dark-coloured four-wheel-drive, mud-caked monsters, sporting the occasional crumpled fender, caused by one too many encounters with a log truck or a roadside tree; CB radio antennas swinging wildly on the rooftops; and in the back, which is sometimes missing a tailgate, an upright fuel barrel and a wooden rack holding two or more proud-looking "working-man" chainsaws, blade down in a vertical position. And behind the wheel, a grizzly, hard-headed, hard-hatted logger, bleary-eyed and gripping the steering wheel while peering over the dash of the truck, heaped with cigarette packages, chainsaw files, bottles of fly dope, and a thermos lying beside a bacon sandwich left over from a 4:30 a.m. breakfast—and ready to take on the day!

It has been said that you can tell a lot about a man by the way he piles his firewood out behind the house. If the pile is straight and the blocks are flush, chances are that he is also neat and well organized. Of course, the opposite also applies.

It follows that loggers can also be sized up by what they have in the large utility boxes carried in the back of their pickup trucks—and how neatly, or not so neatly, they are organized. There would always be the standard stuff—shovels, axes, booster cables, grease guns, and lengths of chain—but it was the unusual stuff that always intrigued me. Items such as half a moose antler; a homemade moose call made from a coffee can and a chunk of rope; an oil-stained, two-year-old copy of *Playboy* magazine that Momma wouldn't find, unless she was looking for a tire wrench. There may have been a battered old, grease-covered fishing tackle box, a blackened, bent-out-of shape tea pail, and maybe even a couple of plastic grocery bags doing double duty as file folders for important papers.

In a way, this chapter is like the loggers' toolboxes. It goes beyond the standard stuff about loggers and lumbermen who worked in Algonquin Park, and is instead an assortment of odds and ends—stories of unique experiences and reflections of my time with the loggers of Algonquin.

When I left Whitney, I thought that I would probably never return. That was not to be, as during more than twenty-five years of employment with the AFA in Pembroke, I estimate that I drove on Highway 60 through Whitney and Algonquin Park more than 900 times.

The trips were frequently early in the morning and in the evenings, and as I have boasted to friends many times, there was not one trip that I didn't enjoy, though road conditions made the trip challenging and even dangerous at times.

There was always something different to marvel at, with the changing of the seasons and the magnificence of the various wildlife. The arrival of moose in the spring months to lick up the roadside salt puddles was especially enthralling. It was necessary to be extra alert at the wheel, as during that time of year as many as fifteen moose were commonly killed by road traffic. On any given trip in the spring, it was not unusual to see ten or more moose between the east and west park gates. I have come across a number of accidents involving moose, none of which was serious to the occupants of the vehicles, but were usually fatal to the unfortunate animals.

There were numerous other road accidents, which did not involve animals, but none as unforgettable as the time I rescued two unusual occupants from their overturned car. The incident occurred on Highway 60 at the top of the Brewer Lake Hill, not far from the park's east gate.

It was a bitterly cold November morning following a night of freezing rain, and the roads were ice-covered and extremely dangerous. I was on my way to a meeting in Dorset, and while passing through Whitney can recall debating the advisability of pulling up and waiting to follow a sand truck through the park. However, since it was an important meeting, I decided to drive on.

As I rounded the turn at the top of the unsanded hill and began to descend, I could see a car upset in the ditch. After much difficulty in stopping my truck safely, I ran to the rescue of the passengers, who were still in the vehicle. The ditch was strewn with female paraphernalia—clothing, bikinis, high-heeled shoes, and even a guitar. As I approached the car, I was greeted by a barrage of profanities such as I have never heard in all my years of working with loggers and lumbermen. It would have made the loggers and sawmillers at Rock Lake blush and run for the hills.

I crawled on my hands and knees through an open front door and pulled out two attractive young women. One was a six-foot blonde, the other a brunette, who looked even taller. Long, lean, and mean is the description that comes to mind.

They were in shock. Upon closer examination, I found that they were relatively uninjured, with the exception of the blonde. She had a nasty gash on her knee that I would have to patch up. And, how would I go about doing that? I had administered first aid to injured loggers before, but never to a six-foot blonde. Actually, it wasn't all that difficult!

They were shivering with the cold, but were able to walk. As I helped them over to the warmth of my truck, and the first-aid kit, the brunette screamed, while pointing to her badly damaged car, lying upside down in the ditch, "Where is the damned sand truck? If I get my hands on that son-of-a-whore-of-a-truck-driver, I'll string the bastard up by his nuts. Look at my car. I just spent $300 on a brake job, and now it is totalled."

It was around 8 a.m. and, as we didn't have a radio system in our vehicles at the time, I was unable to call for help. We had to wait for help to arrive. Finally, a Ministry of Natural Resources employee appeared on the scene and offered to send out the police and a wrecker from Whitney.

As we were sitting in my truck waiting for the police, the brunette spotted the sand truck coming down the hill behind us. She bolted out of my truck, waved her arms like a madwoman, and ran towards the truck yelling, "You goddamned prick. Where were you a half hour ago? Look at my car. I'll kill you, you bastard."

The driver slowed down, rolled down his window, and either couldn't stop, or didn't want to. He kept on driving. He may never know what a good decision that was!

After a few minutes, the blonde said to me, "Son-of-a-bitch. I'm feeling tough. I need a shot of something. Do you have any booze or a smoke or something?" Just at that moment, AFA road foreman Dave Barras came along. Dave smoked small cigars, and he gave them each one. As they sat there, puffing away, filling up the cab of my truck with smoke, we began asking them some questions.

They were from Toronto and were driving to "Egerville," as they called it or, as it more correctly turned out to be, Eganville. They were entertainers and had been engaged to perform at Rooney's Bar in Eganville. Their first performance was scheduled for that afternoon.

I had observed a guitar lying next to their car in the ditch, and very innocently asked them, "Are you singers?"

The brunette replied with a grin, "Well, we can sing a little, but mostly we dance—sometimes on stage and other times on tables." I should have guessed. They were strippers.

I can still see Barras rolling on the ground like a crazy man at my naive question. However, as I left the scene that morning, I couldn't help but think to myself that strippers are just like the rest of us. They have to get up in the morning and drive to work to pay the bills and install new brakes on their car—and, sometimes, their day just doesn't go very well.

When I arrived home that night, I suggested to Heather that we drive out to Rooney's Bar in Eganville to see if those poor girls made it to work. "Not tonight," she replied. "Maybe another time. You have had enough excitement for one day!"

Recently friends of ours gave Heather and me a remarkable book. It is entitled *Reflections of a Century* and was published by the *Eganville Leader*, a remarkable and long-standing weekly newspaper serving the community and region. The book features stories and photographs that were published in the paper from 1902 to 2002.

While browsing through the book one day, I found it, dated November 11, 1987: "Exotic Dancers Flip Car in Algonquin Park." So now you know. I was there—in fact, I was the first one there. An Algonquin experience with a difference!

There were some other "on the road again" adventures on Highway 60 in the park, but far too numerous to mention them all. However, during the many trips through the park, especially in the winter, it was common not to meet a single vehicle between Whitney and Oxtonque Lake on the west side of the park. If it was early in the morning, I amused myself by tuning in a Toronto radio station and listening to the description of the drive-in snarl-up of traffic on the Don Valley Parkway.

Pandemonium for sure, and here I was aching to meet a vehicle around the next turn—and a friendly driver to wave at. Usually it was either moose or wolves. So it has been with great delight that I have described those trips to my two brothers-in-law, Ken MacTavish and Gord Bateman, when they lived in Oakville and Burlington respectively and worked in downtown Toronto. They were both battle-scarred from years of getting on and off GO trains and buses, and not amused by the accounts of my lonely commutes.

One cold dark winter morning, Don McRae and I were driving to work at Rock Lake. Don, who was not a man to waste time, was driving. We were making good time, until we rounded a corner near the Rock Lake turn and came across a pack of wolves, probably six or eight, in the middle of the road. Don was unable to brake as the road was snow- and ice-packed. We ran right over the top of them and could hear the bumping sound of the animals striking the bottom of the truck. We ended up in the snowbank with the wolves disappearing into the bush, apparently unhurt.

On another occasion, I was driving to Huntsville one evening, shortly after the Christmas holidays, during a heavy snowstorm. Near Smoke Lake, I spotted a car buried full length in the snowbank and a young couple standing in the middle of the road, frantically waving their arms for me to stop.

It was obvious they had been there for some time. They didn't have a shovel, so could do nothing but wait for help. A quick look indicated that I couldn't pull them out; a heavy vehicle or tow truck was needed.

I told them to jump in with me, and we would figure something out. The young woman was sobbing, and her equally young husband was just plain scared. They had only been married for a couple of months and were on their way home to Barrie, after having spent the holidays with relatives in Ottawa.

The first question the young fellow asked me was, "We don't have much more than the price of gas to get home. How much do you think it is going to cost to get a tow truck away the hell out here?"

I thought, "What to do?" I wasn't sure!

It was snowing harder than ever without any sign of a plow. In those days, the section of Highway 60 through the park was the last to be attended to. There was not much traffic, especially at night.

And then I remembered that Hay & Company was operating a logging camp in the park near the West Gate, not far off the highway. I didn't know if they had resumed work after the holidays, but drove in to see. Smoke was coming out of the chimneys and there were lights on. I told my passengers to remain in the truck, and I went into the foreman's shack.

There were three men sitting around on their bunks, puffing on pipes and undoubtedly telling tall tales. I explained the situation and that my young friends had no money. Within an instant, they all jumped out of their chairs, eager to help.

The camp foreman, whose name I cannot recall, asked if they had eaten supper. I told him probably not. In a flash, he was out the door and heading towards the cookery where the old cook and cookee were cleaning up after supper. Within minutes, they had assembled leftovers from supper—and presented their young guests with a piping-hot roast beef feast, complete with mashed potatoes, gravy, vegetables, homemade bread, and raisin pie.

The foreman told them that they could spend the night in the camp, if they wished. However, he would send his snowplow truck to pull them out right away, as they had to go in that direction to plow out a logging road close by for the log trucks on the night shift.

"Don't worry," he told the young couple. "We have to drive right by your car, so put your money away." However, the foreman avoided eye contact with me. He knew, that I knew, that was a fabrication. Their logging and hauling operations weren't even remotely close to the stranded vehicle.

As I left for home that night, the couple was cleaning up their second piece of pie, their faces beaming as if it were Christmas all over again. Here's to you and your men, Mr. Foreman!

Stories such as this, as remarkable as they are, were commonplace in those days. Loggers and log-truck drivers have always been well known for helping out stranded motorists.

A few weeks later I found myself in the reverse situation, on the receiving end of some kindness. I was driving to work at Rock Lake from Huntsville early one bitterly cold Saturday morning. It was an almost unbearable minus thirty-five-degree day. About 6 a.m., the fan belt on my truck broke near the entrance to the Tea Lake campsite. The phone in a nearby booth was not working. I could do nothing but wait for a passerby.

To keep warm I took my axe, which I always carried with me, and waded through the snow to find an old pine stump, which I dragged out into the centre of the road. No motorist was going to drive by me without stopping. In the meantime, I made and tended a huge fire on the white line of Highway 60. Another Algonquin Park first!

Three hours later, at 9 a.m., I could hear the sound of a vehicle approaching from the east. Around the corner chugged a beat-up old multi-coloured Volkswagen Beetle. I could barely see the driver. He was crouched down over the wheel peering out a small opening in the corner of the windshield, which he kept clear by scraping the frost with his fingernails. Volkswagen cars in those days were engineered to generate little or no heat.

The car stopped and out jumped a young black man with a huge gap-toothed grin. He had a Montreal Canadiens toque pulled down over his ears and was wearing an army parka—and knee-high, white flight boots. He was dressed for the high Arctic and probably thought that he had arrived there.

With an easily recognizable Maritime accent, he chuckled as he rubbed his hands, "Some frigging frigid—wha?" And then asked, "Are you having trouble, mate, or were you just waiting for me to come along before you started roasting the hot dogs—wha?"

He was a soldier from Camp Petawawa and also a professional boxer driving to Toronto to compete in a lightweight fight that night. I jumped in with him, and he had me in stitches all the way to Huntsville. He drove me to a garage and insisted on driving me back to my vehicle, but I declined and called a friend.

I crack up every time I think about that guy. Maybe, in some small way, he has something to do with the soft spot that I have for military people—not to mention the affection that I feel towards Maritimers. What a tonic he was for someone having a bad start to their day—wha!

The early morning trips on Highway 60 were the best. It was then that the kids were huddled at the side of the road waiting for school buses, laughing and pushing and shoving each other, with their backpacks, ball gloves, and hockey sticks scattered all over the ditch. Often, a tail-wagging family dog would be in the middle of it all.

I would make an effort to smile and wave at them as I passed, sometimes even blowing the horn. They would be quick to return the waves. Over the years, I looked forward to seeing them at the usual spots, some of my favourites being the top of the big hill at Madawaska, the village of Round Lake, and some homes a few miles east of Whitney.

I could tell that some of them recognized me from previous trips, and it was interesting to observe the changes in each kid from year to year. It was as if we were getting to know each other.

I would miss seeing them during the summer months and marvel at how much they had grown when they appeared again in September. Each year, there were some new little ones and others who were not there anymore, probably having moved on to "the other side." Some were undoubtedly working in nearby sawmills, or in the bush on a logging operation with their dads. The girls were probably off to big-city jobs, or getting ready to raise some kids of their own, not far from grannie's watchful and caring eye.

"Ask for Red Man chewing tobacco and hurry up. Don't drive too fast, and bring me back the goddamned change."

—Delbert MacTavish Sr., logger, cattle trader, and horseman

In close to forty years of working with loggers and lumbermen, I have met only two men who were quite like J.S.L. McRae. One was Johnnie Shaw of Herb Shaw & Sons in Pembroke (you will hear more about him later), the other was my father-in-law, Delbert MacTavish. Delbert descended from a long line of hardy Scots. He was a tough-minded, frugal, no-nonsense man with a crusty exterior, cleverly masking a huge tender spot that we all knew was there.

Delbert was raised on a small farm in Harrington, Quebec. At the age of sixteen, he bought a team of horses and went logging in the shanties north of Harrington. He used to tell us that he made $2 a day—and that included the team and their feed.

He logged for a few winters while buying and selling cattle in the summer months, but his aspirations were aimed at the bright lights. In his twenties, he sold the team of horses and purchased a standardbred racehorse. From that point on, he never looked back.

He went on to become a successful and well-known trainer, driver, and owner of standardbred racehorses in Canada and the U.S. He is a member of the Canadian Harness Racing Hall of Fame and, in 2001, we attended his induction into the Saratoga Raceway Hall of Fame in Saratoga Springs, New York.

Delbert was a successful businessman and horseman, not only due to his ability to understand and handle a horse, but also due to the manner that he sized up people. The first test when meeting him was to be able to look him straight in the eye—and survive the grip of a mighty handshake. He shook hands like he was pulling a stuck heifer out of a swamp.

His customary poker face rarely conjured up a smile, except when on the giving end of a practical joke—all hell would break loose when he found himself on the receiving end of one. He was once described by a Montreal sportscaster as being a "dour Scotsman, who talks softly and carries a big stick."

Delbert and his wife Bunty spent many winters in Deleon Springs, Florida, where he trained his racehorses. They would come back to Montreal or Saratoga Springs each year for the summer racing season.

He once told me that upon arriving in Saratoga one spring, he went for a haircut, the barber being a long-time friend. They were so happy to see each other that Delbert shook his hand hard enough to break the barber's little finger. He felt badly about that, although the barber had more pain and discomfort out of the incident than he did.

I had been his son-in-law for twenty-six years when he passed away in 1994, and although Delbert and I had an excellent relationship, I don't recall him ever calling me by my first name. It was either "Whatchmacallit" or "Charlie McCarthy." The shanties and racetrack paddocks had more Willies, Joes, and Petes than relatively modern names like mine. It amused me that he could not call me Brent.

Delbert had a long association in the horseracing business with former Montreal Canadien hockey player and enforcer, John Ferguson. He and Bunty became good friends with John, his wife Joan, and their family.

John was from British Columbia and, due to the rigours of the NHL schedule, was usually unable to return home for special times like Thanksgiving and Christmas. On these holidays, they were often invited to the MacTavish farm near Brownsburg, Quebec.

On one such occasion, a few of us were playing cards and coaxing Ferguson to comment on a recent Canadiens' coaching change. It was either Al MacNeil or Claude Ruel, I can't remember which. It was John's turn to deal. In contrast to his usual "man-of-few-words" demeanour, he became carried away with the explanation, causing a delay in the dealing of the cards.

Delbert listened impatiently for a short time before finally shouting, "Quit your yapping, Ferguson, and deal the goddamned cards." I have yet to meet another man who would have said that to John Ferguson—certainly not one standing in a pair of skates.

Delbert's ability to judge character was effective and dead-eye simple. There were only two types of men as far as he was concerned. You were either "not a bad fella" or a "common son-of-a-whore." Heather, our daughter Kathy, and I were with him when he passed away. I like to think that he had me in the former category.

The annual Loggers Day celebration is a major attraction held in Algonquin Park every summer on a Saturday near the end of July. The park's Logging Museum is the setting for the event, which is supported jointly by the AFA, Ontario Parks, and the Friends of Algonquin. Each year, one thousand visitors enjoy a fun-filled and informative day intended to provide them with a glimpse at past logging practices—and an increased awareness of current practices.

Park naturalists Dan Strickland and Ron Tozer, dressed in period clothing, are there to explain how the authentic "cadge crib" and "alligator boat" were used to move timber across large lakes, the timber eventually reaching fast-moving rivers for transfer to downstream markets.

Logger Hans Koster, from Bancroft, Ontario, is the only modern-day man that we know of who has figured out the configuration and function of the multitude of wheels, brakes, and cable making up the "crazy wheel." It is more correctly known as the Barrienger brake, presumably after its inventor. It is a strange-looking, stationary piece of equipment used to safely ease sleigh-loads of logs down steep hills in the winter. Hans is always a big hit with visitors, and eagerly awaits this opportunity each year to explain how his "pet" works.

Elva Gorgerat, relaxing at her confectionary and lunch bar in Whitney.

Equally as popular is forester Tom "Jigger" Stephenson, who demonstrates his collection of log-stamping hammers and provides kids with actual hands-on experience in manufacturing rope. Tom, with his bright red hair and huge smile, is easily picked out of a crowd when he participates in the pioneer section of countless international plowing matches throughout Ontario.

Forester Ray Townsend, who designed the log-driving dam at the museum, is there with his hearty laugh and crazy hat highlighting his "Joe Mufferaw" outfit, and to explain how the dam was used by the pioneer log-driving crews.

A swarm of kids can always be found at the site of the crosscut sawing contests intended for the enjoyment of "wannabe loggers."

Visitors can laugh and dance at performances in the camboose camp by the Wakami Wailers, with their fiddles, guitars, outlandish attire, and shanty songs.

The highlight of the day for most is the loggers' working-man meal, prepared by a local legend, Elva Gorgerat of Whitney. Elva is an outstanding cook and has cooked many meals for hungry loggers over the years. At the time of writing, she and her husband Ed had a small confectionary store and lunch bar in the heart of Whitney. She is a treat to visit if you are passing that way.

The camp meal is provided to visitors for a nominal cost. It is served at noon in the museum's cookery and lasts until the food runs out. The cookery was built to replicate the standard McRae Lumber Co. cookery design. It is authentic, right down to the location of the pantry and cookstove. The stovepipes are in the same position as they were when Jack McRae and I took measurements on a dark night at the Lemon Lake camp in 1963.

With her usual friendly grin, Elva presides over the serving of a feast of baked beans, sausages, bologna, homemade bread, fried potatoes, slices of side pork floating in a sea of grease, hot biscuits, camp cookies, and butter tarts to die for. It is enough to bring the cholesterol police storming out of the hills, but absolutely delicious, nevertheless.

Elva could also stand her ground with the toughest of loggers. I experienced one example of her determination while we were setting things up for the first Loggers Day event in 1995. It was a new venture and we had a few bugs to work out in the layout of the various displays.

A display tent was erected too close to the access road leading to the cookery. I was in another location on site and looked up to see John Haskins running towards me, waving his arms: "Elva wants to see you right away."

As I approached her sitting in a van loaded full of food, she motioned to the tent, which was blocking her access, and she remarked with a huge grin, "If you want me to feed anybody today, I am going to have to drive through your son-of-a-whore of a tent." The tent was relocated within minutes.

At another Loggers Day, Gary Cannon and I were sitting together at one of the tables in the cookery, enjoying Elva's meal. We were chatting and reminiscing about our times working together, and marvelling at the authenticity of the McRae cookery. Even the huge breadbox was in the same place—it even appeared to be the same box, which we had both seen Gary's uncle Tommy fill with fresh loaves after they had been removed from the hot oven.

As we talked, I spotted a young boy sitting across from us, probably twelve years of age. He was watching us intently, taking in every word. Finally, he approached and asked, "Gee, are you guys real-life loggers?"

"Yes, we are son, and mighty proud of it. What would you like to know?" replied Gary, with his big smile and larger-than-life voice.

For the next twenty minutes, we held court with some historical descriptions and yarns, some factual, others stretched a bit. The young lad's family joined us, as did another family, and we had to have our pictures taken with each group. Gary was in his element, swinging his arms like a windmill and having the time of his life.

As I think about my friend Gary, who has since passed away, I like to think that somewhere, perhaps working in a Toronto high-rise, there is a young man who can say, "One time, when I was a little guy, I made friends with two real-life Algonquin Park loggers."

In sharing some of the stories in this chapter I realize I have digressed from the central focus on the loggers of Algonquin, and a professional editor would probably be justified in scolding me gently for doing so. However, I have found that most loggers I have known have similar tendencies. During nightly storytelling sessions in the bunkhouse, the range of subjects could swing wildly from the towering white pine tree missed by J.R. Booth crews in the 1930s to the friendly Canada jay taking flight from a lunch bucket, beak loaded with a dill pickle and an untouched bologna sandwich made from two-inch-thick slices of homemade bread. Now, I promise to refocus. As best I can.

Chapter 4—Tales of Truck Drivers

"You could put all the sand that the good-for-nothing, son-of-a-bitch of a sand truck driver spread on that hill into your mouth, and you wouldn't even taste the grit."

—Ab Hoffman, truck driver, Lake Superior Park

It was as if Sault Ste. Marie and Weyerhaeuser Canada Ltd. were at opposite ends of the planet from Whitney and McRae Lumber. No longer was it Hockey Night in Whitney, every night of the week on a numbing cold, windswept outdoor rink. We were now in the midst of an elaborate National Hockey League spawning bed, producing such well-known players as Phil and Tony Esposito, Chico Maki, and Lou Nanne. At the time, a "tad of a lad" named Ron Francis was just barely learning how to tie the laces in his first pair of skates.

The eye-blurring blizzard of one-channel television reception in Whitney had given way to the delirium of cablevision. A local newspaper was delivered daily to the front doorstep. It was no longer necessary to wait a couple of days for a truck driver to bring a paper back to Rock Lake after a trip to Toronto with a load of lumber.

The Weyerhaeuser office swarmed with a gallery of suave, clean-shaven, and cologned accountants, attired in sports jackets and neckties, working on large electronic calculators which, of all things, could multiply and divide as well as add. What a contrast it was to the sight of Paddy Roche working by himself in the Rock Lake office early on a winter morning, cranking on a one-arm adding machine, ruggedly dressed in his wool pants with braces, gum rubbers, and plaid shirt.

Imagine! And there were women working in the office, too! The only time we saw a female at Rock Lake was when a family of campers staying at the park campsite came to the mill looking for slabwood for their campfires.

Weyerhaeuser was then, and still is, a huge, progressive American company, considered to be a leader in the forest industry. It owned more private forest land in the U.S. than any other corporation or individual. The company was headquartered in Tacoma, Washington, and at the time I worked for them had 40,000 employees in many countries.

The Canadian operations consisted of sawmills and veneer mills in Sault Ste. Marie and Mattawa, Ontario, and Princeville, Quebec, and a pulp mill in Kamloops, British Columbia. The Soo mill complex was a modern-equipped operation employing more than 300 workers and supported by substantial financial and management resources—management being largely dominated by Americans, who were parachuted in for brief stays on their rapid ascent up the corporate ladder. During the ten years I was there, two of the four general managers were Americans.

One had to be impressed, however, with the sophisticated methods and modern equipment. I was especially struck by the expensive shiny black and yellow Mack log trucks with piggy-back trailers, which were loaded onto the tandem trucks for the empty trip back to the bush.

However, amidst all this space-age pizzazz, it puzzled me that for a camp foreman to order fifteen dollars worth of stovepipe for the construction of a cookery, it was necessary to complete a five-part purchase order and route the whole thing through a purchasing manager wearing a business suit and a paisley tie. Somehow, I know, Jack McRae, sporting a worn-out cardigan and his stubby pencil, would have had a problem with that!

Yes, there were many differences between the Weyerhaeuser and McRae operations, but the one constant was the loggers. No matter where they work or who they work for, loggers know what it is like to get up early in the morning to do their job, often under extreme hardships and dangerous conditions. These are the same men who will care for an orphaned deer or a displaced or injured bird, and when the day is done, will make you laugh your fool head off in storytelling sessions sitting on the edge of their bunks.

Logger Bob Lemke and his crew were working in the Odenback area of Algonquin Park one winter, when they came across a hibernating bear. Its den had been flooded by an unexpected thaw, terrifying the poor animal. They immediately cordoned off the area, cut some balsam brush to keep the bear dry, and called for the park biologist to come with his staff to help relocate or comfort the bear.

Another time in Algonquin, a cutter inadvertently cut down a tree that contained a hawk's nest. The nest was not readily visible in a dense crown of branches and had been previously missed by the tree markers, otherwise, it would have been protected. The cutter and his skidder operator valiantly stood the tree back up against another tree with the skidder, hoping to undo the damage. It was not the right thing to do from a safety aspect, but credit must go to these men for trying to do the best they could for the hawk and her family.

It is stories like these that go mainly untold during blurts of anti-logging rhetoric. It is my hope that by sharing them with you, there will be a somewhat better appreciation for the professionalism of these fine men.

Someday, I will tell you about some of the amazing loggers that I worked with in Lake Superior Park and in Mattawa, Ontario, while working for Weyerhaeuser. In the meantime, I can't resist the opportunity to jump the gun a bit, to reflect and share some stories of the truck drivers that I have known in Algonquin and Lake Superior Parks.

My first job with Weyerhaeuser was to locate new logging roads on the ground, usually in areas that were undeveloped and had no previous road systems.

This was my first glimpse into the psychology of a truck driver, and the wild notions and exaggerations that they are known for. Truck drivers are in a class by themselves. They live and breathe driving trucks, and are genetically modified and hard-wired to complain and entertain—eager to tell far-fetched stories about their hauling escapades—at the drop of a hat.

They spend so much time behind the wheel by themselves, thinking, that it is little wonder that they have something to say about almost anything. Their favourite commentary is to analyse why a logging road was located where it was, and who was the dummy that located and built it there in the first place. Of course, their evaluation would come from the comfort of a plush Boston air-lift seat, inside a stereo-equipped, air-conditioned truck cab.

In all my years, I have yet to see a truck driver stumbling around in a swamp, or crawling along a side hill on his hands and knees, with a packsack on his back, trying to find the best location for a logging road.

However, I have never met a log truck driver that I didn't like. Their simple charm and good humour far outshine the blather!

First of all, it is unlikely a truck driver would be overheard saying, "Oh my goodness gracious, it sure would be nice to meet the amazing chap who did such a good job engineering the side-cut over that big hill. That gentle grade is an outstanding piece of work. It's a heavenly pleasure to drive my truck over roads like that."

Instead, one would be more apt to hear, "Boy, would I ever like to get my hands around the neck of the stupid rotten son-of-a-whore who put that frigging road up over that gobbler's knob. It will take a bulldozer pulling me and one pushing to get up that hill—and when I do, I will need to get hooked up to an oxygen tank to stay alive."

And then there is the prospect of sitting at the head table of a wedding party, next to the groom. If he were a truck driver, this is a sample of what he might say until the bride had thrown away her garter and was ready for the honeymoon to get underway back at the hotel room.

"By Jeez, I was hauling logs one night in a blinding snowstorm, Inbacka Mackey . . ."

It took me a long time to discover that there was no such place as Inbacka Mackey. Instead, there was a scattering of houses on Highway 17 along the Ottawa River between Deep River and Mattawa. The settlement was called Mackey. The local loggers in the Upper Ottawa Valley regularly referred to any area west of Mackey and stretching to the Manitoba border as Inbacka Mackey.

"Yes, sir, the snow was as thick as a gallon of warm buttermilk in a three-quart jar—couldn't even see the bulldog on the hood of my Mack. I had a big load of pine on her, and double-clutched and split-shifted that old girl to the highway in less than an hour—and without chains. I passed the sand truck upset on its side in the ditch at mile twenty. Didn't see the snowplow once—son-of-a-bitch of a driver was probably back at the camp fooling around with the cook.

"Yes, siree! I arrived in the sawmill yard in Mattawa two hours before the loader man's wife had forked the breakfast bacon out of the frying pan—and that's the honest-to-God's truth."

Some will comment how fast log-truck drivers drive on the highway. This is well summed up in an observation made by my all-time favourite comedian, Cape Breton-raised Ron James. He suggests to truckers, "Slow down, you bastards—it's only wood—it will keep."

I am reminded about the time that I ordered a load of top soil for our garden from a trucker when we lived in Pembroke. A week went by and the load didn't show up. Finally, he called me one night to check on where I lived. He must have been working overtime at happy hour, because he was happy as a clam. I told him that we lived on Elizabeth Street, a "stone's throw" from the Civic Hospital. He replied with a chuckle and a slur, "A 'stone's throw' you say! Now, don't you be breaking any frigging windows. Heh, heh."

Duncan MacGregor told me a story once about one of the McGuey boys from Whitney, who drove a truck many years for McRae. He had been in a trucking accident, injuring his back, and was confined to the Barry's Bay hospital. He was strapped to a huge board, which extended several inches beyond the width of his shoulders. He was able to walk around, but not very comfortably, as the hallways of the hospital were quite narrow.

One day, after having too much of the hospital's ragout the night before, he developed a bad case of the runs. He had to make an emergency visit to the washroom. As he raced down the hall, he met head-on with an old fellow nonchalantly rolling up the hall in a wheelchair. There was no way that they could pass without colliding, so McGuey screamed at him, "Turn out you son-of-a-bitch, turn out, or I'll run over you!"

Weyerhaeuser's logging supervisors, foresters, and timber cruisers were normally assigned standard-sized pickup trucks for their work. However, with increasing fleet maintenance costs, a decision was made, probably at the insistence of some disconnected accountants, to sell all the trucks when their useful life expired and replace them with Volkswagen Beetles. At the time, the Beetle had a nominal capital cost of $1,900.

And that is when the fun began! The Beetles were fine for highway travel, but in addition to having very low ground clearance, they just could not stand up to the punishment of driving on bush roads. Besides, the foremen couldn't haul any supplies, such as oil barrels and winch cable.

The greatest difficulty, however, was during the winter months, when roadside snowbanks were as high as eight or ten feet. Truckers hated the Volkswagens, as they couldn't see the cars approaching them around curves on narrow logging roads. There were numerous near misses and a couple of minor collisions as a result.

In those days, there was not the benefit of CB radios, as there is on modern-day logging operations, where all vehicles travelling in the bush are required to have one on board. Mileage markers are located at every mile of bush road and drivers call out their location on channel 19, as they drive in or out of the logging operations. "Coming in empty at mile twenty," will often be followed by a response like, "Coming out loaded at mile twenty-two."

Usually one of the vehicles, most commonly the lighter half-tons, will pull over to allow the loaded truck to pass safely. Heaven help the driver who fails to call out his location; he may find himself face-to-face with the business end of a seventy-ton loaded log truck. Or what may be even worse, the receiving end of a pissed-off truck driver.

The problem with the Volkswagens headed the agenda of many company safety committee meetings. A recommended improvement was the installation of ten-foot whip aerials, with orange flags on the top, to be mounted on the rear bumper of the cars.

Now that was a sight to behold! I was standing on the top of a hill one day talking to truck driver Ab Hoffman, and as we looked down over a series of side-cuts in the road far below us, we could see a moving orange flag barely visible over the top of the snowbanks. It was a real treat to hear Ab growl, "Look at that, another one of those goddamned road runners with a flag pole sticking out of its arse, looking to get squashed. Real loggers drive a truck in the bush, not a frigging stocking stuffer." Needless to say, the Volkswagen experiment was short-lived.

One day while working for the AFA, amidst a particularly heated controversy over logging in Algonquin Park, I received a call from Kelly Egan, a well-known feature writer for the *Ottawa Citizen*. He was planning on writing an article about the subject and asked if I could help him understand the issues.

A tour was arranged, and on one sunny June morning, I drove him into the park to see some logging operations first-hand. At the end of the day, we were driving towards Pembroke and, while rounding a curve on a main logging road, found a huge snapping turtle in the middle of it.

In May and June, turtles are frequently found laying eggs in the soft gravel on the shoulder of the roads, and truck drivers do their best to avoid running over them. And now, it was showtime for my reporter friend!

Since there was a lot of traffic on the road that day, I stopped my truck and with a round-mouthed shovel tried to move the turtle. It had been attempting to cross the road into a swamp on the other side. With our arrival, it stopped moving and did a good impression of a stone. The turtle was a dead weight of about twenty-five pounds and was not being very co-operative, standing her ground with everything tucked under the massive shell.

As Kelly and I worked frantically to move the turtle, we could hear the sound of an approaching truck coming out of the park. In a few minutes, a tractor-trailer loaded with logs appeared, slowed down, and with the hiss of its air brakes, came to a stop.

Out jumped the driver, Herbie Hass, whom I knew well and who, along with other loggers working in the park, would be very much aware of the public spotlight shining on logging in the park.

He approached us with his usual huge grin and asked, "Do you boys want me to charm that big snapper for you?" I introduced Kelly to Herbie, and Kelly appeared to be impressed with the fact that a truck driver would stop his big rig just to save the life of a lowly turtle, and he said so to Herbie.

"Hell," Herbie said, "us truckers have nightmares at the thought of running over a poor turtle. We would run our trucks into the ditch, if need be, to miss hitting one. Why, just last week, I prit' near lost a half hour waiting for one of those suckers to finish tanning herself and get off the road before I could continue on to the mill."

Kelly took a couple of pictures, and as we drove to town, he told me that he would like to include the incident in his article, providing he had space and agreement from his editor. In a week or so, the feature article appeared in the *Citizen*. With his usual high standard of observation and description, Kelly had presented a well-balanced report of the issues. However, the turtle story didn't make it. I suppose the editor may have thought that Herbie's comments were a little far-fetched. I can't really say if they were or not; only good old Herbie would be able to tell us that.

And now it is confession time! I have never told this story, since the incident occurred nearly forty years ago, but if by chance any of the truck drivers who were present that day are still alive, I would like them to know that since I retired I have unfortunately become homeless with no fixed address.

It was during an extremely wet spring in 1966 at Weyerhaeuser's Camp 67, north of Sault Ste. Marie. I was filling in for the road construction foreman who was away for a few days on a fishing trip. Our gravel crew was having difficulty keeping the logging crews serviced with roads, because it was so wet. Consequently, we were working fifteen-hour days to keep ahead.

The crew consisted of five truck drivers, a loader operator, and a dozer operator to spread the gravel. I can't remember all the individuals in the crew, but do recall two-hard-working drivers named Ron and Don. They had both worked in Algonquin Park and were now operating two trucks as Ron and Don Haulage.

The other trucker was Shorty Stevens from Wilberforce, Ontario. He was one of the best-known truckers in the business. I had known Shorty for many years, having hired him to haul logs for me while I was in Mattawa and Pembroke. Whenever I needed to hire him, it was a simple matter to reach him by calling the operator and asking for Wilberforce 6. Everybody knew Shorty's phone number. He was a feisty little guy with a big smile, always ready to editorialize about the state of the trucking business. He could always be counted on to be the first truck to arrive in the morning and the last one to leave with a load at night.

The crew was working about fifteen miles from the main Mile 67 camp. Each day, I would drive into the camp around five o'clock to pick up a hot supper for the men. This enabled them to keep on working and not be delayed by having to drive into the camp for supper. We had a small batch-trailer located in the gravel pit, which was equipped with a propane stove to reheat the food.

One day I was running a little behind schedule picking up the meal. I had to make some stops to see the clerk in the office and the mechanic in the garage, so it was late by the time I got to the cookery. "I would have to hustle to make it back to the gravel pit for the usual meal time of six," I thought.

The cook had an excellent meal ready, wrapped in newspapers to keep it warm. It consisted of two small pails of boiled potatoes and vegetables, and a huge steaming-hot pot of liver stew, swimming with onions, mushrooms, and carrots. It smelled delicious, if you had a taste for liver.

I placed the meal on the seat of my truck and took off, driving as fast as I could. I was about three miles from the gravel pit, and as I went around a sharp turn in the road . . . you guessed it. Over went the pot of stew onto the floorboards of the truck.

I was able to grab the pot, so that it didn't all spill, but most of it was lying in the sand on the floor. What to do? Panic didn't set in, but it was close. Then the answer came. It was too far and too late to return to the camp for more, so I drove up the road to a small spring creek and carefully washed the pieces of liver in the cool clear waters of the creek and returned them to the pot.

I arrived at the trailer before the men did, heated up the meal, and left it on the stove for them to help themselves. In a few minutes they arrived and, while washing up, commented on the delicious aroma coming from the pot of liver stew. They heaped up their plates and, within seconds, I could hear the grinding sounds of their teeth and see the painful grimaces come over their faces.

Shorty jumped out of his chair, dumped his meal into a nearby garbage pail, and yelped, "That goddamned cook. Does he think we are a bunch of roosters with gizzards? There is more gravel on my plate than I hauled out of the pit all forenoon. I am going to strangle that old bastard when I get back to the camp tonight, damn it all to hell!"

I had to leave the trailer and go outside, so I could laugh freely. The meal that night was potatoes and carrots, with warm raisin pie for dessert. And until this day, I have never told the men that it wasn't the cook's fault. I was the one to blame, and I have been swimming around in a sea of guilt all these years.

My story does have a footnote, however, that helped me stay off the hook at the time. The cook was an unreliable, miserable old coot who was constantly fighting with the men. At the time of this incident, camp foreman Roy Perkins had already decided to replace him with another cook at the end of the month.

Chapter 5—A Personal Moment

"The best years of your life are when the kids are old enough to shovel the driveway, but too young to drive the car."

—Bits and Pieces

Algonquin Park loggers, lumbermen, and other park workers were a very important part of my life; many of them became and remain close friends. But where to draw the line? At times, I struggle when writing about them in this book, recognizing that this should be about them and not me. However, I am unable to disconnect them completely from my own life, and feel compelled to share some of my personal circumstances with you. I hope that you will not find it presumptuous.

A marriage, which had been on shaky ground during my time with McRae's, finally failed completely within two years of our arrival in Sault Ste. Marie. The future looked pretty bleak. There were three young children involved, and thankfully family members jumped in to help us out. My mother and father, George and Marion Connelly of Brownsburg, Quebec, and an aunt and uncle, Kathleen and Emerson Noble of Lachute, Quebec, cared for the kids until we were able to get back onto our feet.

My parents were well known in their community for reaching out to others, frequently driving people without transportation to services at their church in Lachute. My mother, who was a Grade 1 teacher in Brownsburg, had met a young mother who was living and working in Brownsburg. Like me, she was raising three young children from a previous marriage.

The young lady was the former Heather MacTavish from Lachute, and my mother had taught two of her kids. As a teenager, I had known her older brother Duncan, against whom I had played hockey. I did not know Heather personally, although, as she was one of the prettiest girls in Lachute, I knew who she was.

I was in Brownsburg one weekend and found myself in the Margaret Roger Memorial Presbyterian Church in Lachute with my family for the Sunday morning service. Much to my delight, I discovered Heather sitting in a pew not too far away, having been driven there earlier by my father.

After the service, my parents explained with an apology that they had to attend a meeting and could not take Heather and her family home. Would my little red station wagon be able to accommodate Heather and all the kids for the drive home to Brownsburg?

The Connelly Family, Lachute, Quebec,
October 12, 1968.
Left to right: Michael, Brent, John, Mom,
Dad, Kathy, Christine, Janet.

"Not a problem," I insisted. "We'll just have to snuggle up a little, that's all." At that moment, my little red Acadian station wagon, with the small jump seat in the back, was big enough to drive the entire Dallas Cowboys football team across the state of Texas and back.

And that was the first day of a love story that is as wonderful now as it was then.

In October of 1968, Heather and I were married in the same church where we met. Our six children—Janet age nine; Michael and Brent, seven; Christine and Kathy, six; and John, five—were our attendants, as they stood next to us at the front of the church throughout the service. A few months later the process was completed when Heather and I adopted each other's children.

A year later on Halloween night, our new family received a "treat" in the form of baby Nancy. This was followed by a busy time of fun and challenge, which included three years with six teenagers in the house. There would have been no survivors, if Heather had not stayed at home to preside over all the action! Later came eleven grandchildren to love, laugh with, and marvel at.

Over the years, I frequently teased my mother about the masterful job of matchmaking that she and my father had pulled off. She would neither confirm nor deny any involvement, but that sly little smile, as she turned away to avoid eye contact, told it all.

There is a little bit of everything in this story: romance, adventure, camping trips, children's laughter, and even some irony. My mother passed away in 2003 in her ninety-first year. Her funeral was held in the same Presbyterian church where Heather and I had met and were married. The date was October 12, exactly thirty-five years to the day since our wedding.

Somehow, it seems fitting that we were able to celebrate her remarkable life on the same day as our wedding anniversary. Whenever my sister Janice and I meet, we reminisce about our parents with great pride, affection, and gratitude. Both are gone now and it is with those same feelings, not sadness, that I enjoy sharing this personal moment.

*Nancy, a family
Halloween treat.*

Chapter 6—The Algonquin Forestry Authority

"We know how many plates are set at the table, but we can't serve the pie until we put our boots on and go to the bush to find out how many pieces there will be—and if it will be lemon meringue or pie in the sky."

—I.D. (Joe) Bird, forester, general manager, Algonquin Forestry Authority

The Weyerhaeuser dream was beginning to fade by the early 1970s. It was obvious that logging in Lake Superior Park would come to an end soon, then a sawmill fire at the Mattawa operation cut short my tenure there and in northeastern regions of Algonquin Park.

For a period the company examined the feasibility of building a pulp mill near Wawa, and I was involved with that briefly. After much sizzle about the prospects of this major expansion, nothing materialized. The explanation given to us was that a "socialist government" at Queen's Park had spooked the decision-makers in the Tacoma, Washington, corporate office.

It was with mixed feelings that, once again, I reached for the résumé file. Our family loved living in Sault Ste. Marie, and I had a good job at the time. However, there was uncertainty written all over the future, and my heart had never really left Algonquin Park. As it turned out, the Soo operation changed hands several times after I left. As I write, it is a shadow of the prominent manufacturing complex that it once was.

I would miss the many fine loggers I worked with in my ten years of employment with Weyerhaeuser. Someday, I hope to return and tell you all about them. At the top of the list of fascinating stories to share is an experience my boss and good friend Tony Vorlicek had in Lake Superior Park. We were travelling by canoe in a remote part of the park and unexpectedly came upon something out of *Alice in Wonderland*. It was a cedar-shake cabin on stilts, well-hidden near the shore of a small wilderness lake, which overflowed with speckled trout. But I digress.

And then our ship came in! In 1974, the forest industry was buzzing with the news: a newly established government agency, the Algonquin Forestry Authority, was being established. It was to take over the logging operations in Algonquin Park and supply forest products to dependent mills surrounding the park.

I.D. (Joe) Bird, forester and
first general manager
of the Algonquin Forestry Authority.

Upon first hearing the news, my colleagues and I grumbled at great length about what an outrageous notion it was to have public servants running logging operations and selling logs to hard-nosed lumbermen, like Jack McRae. How ridiculous! "Holy old whistlin'." The world was coming to an end!

Initially, I paid little heed to the employment ads which first appeared in the *Globe and Mail*. From my vantage, the prospects of this new concept succeeding appeared to be slim.

The Ontario government had appointed a board of directors, comprising ten individuals representing various professions and communities around the park. The board had hired a general manager, I.D. "Joe" Bird, a well-known forester and forestry industry executive, who had worked for many years with the Ontario Paper Company in northern Ontario and eastern Quebec. Joe had only been recently appointed and was working out of a hotel room in Huntsville, putting together his initial staffing plan.

The ads outlined the requirements for an accountant and three foresters, consisting of an operations superintendent in Huntsville and two area supervisors, one in Huntsville and the other in Pembroke. In spite of my scepticism, there was one nagging thought that I couldn't ignore: This was Algonquin Park we were talking about here, which in my mind was every forester's dream. After some encouraging thoughts from Heather and a night of unsettled sleep, I mailed my résumé the following day.

I had heard that the response was substantial and, therefore, was surprised and flattered to receive a call from Joe Bird a couple of weeks later inviting me for an interview the following weekend. As we talked generally on the phone, he made a suggestion, which I thought to be unusual at the time. The reason became clear later on.

"I see from your résumé that you have a house full of kids at home," Joe said. "Why don't you bring your wife down to Huntsville for the weekend to give her a break. We will pay your expenses."

I didn't have to pass that one by Heather twice. Off we went like a couple of honeymooners to the Hidden Valley Resort Hotel on beautiful Peninsula Lake in the heart of Muskoka. The interview was a gruelling two-hour session led by Joe, with several directors also participating. There weren't the usual jitters in the early stages, as I had a good job with Weyerhaeuser and was not really expecting to be a successful candidate. However, after hearing Joe outline his plans, I became very impressed by his businesslike approach, intelligence, quiet enthusiasm, and sheer magnetism. Any possible indifference or doubt that I may have had in the beginning was transformed into a feeling of eagerness to join Joe's team. There was an anticipation of something good about to happen in Algonquin Park. By the end of the interview, the juices were flowing for the first time in a long time.

Later on that afternoon there was a message in our room to call Mr. Bird. He asked if he could join us for dinner in the dining room, and we had an enjoyable meal over friendly conversation about our families and professional experiences.

I can recall commenting to Heather as we went for a walk after dinner in the cool air of an April evening that Joe did exactly what Jack McRae had done over a decade before. Mr. McRae asked what my father and grandfathers did for a living. By inviting Heather, Joe was doing as J.S.L. had done. He wanted a glimpse of the man behind the forester. Heather was his window.

A few days later, Joe called to offer me the job of area supervisor in Pembroke. The next night, Heather and I went out for dinner to celebrate. My toast to her that evening was, "Thanks for doing so well in 'our interview' and congratulations on 'our new job.'"

Joe Bird was a handsome man with a Robert Redford smile and wavy salt-and-pepper hair. He was in good physical condition—he jogged in the mornings—and had been a football hero in his UNB days. He was intelligent, charming and humorous; the kind of man that people gravitate to.

Our first staff meeting was in newly acquired office space in Huntsville in July 1975. We sat on chairs that had been delivered to the office only minutes before. I was introduced to my new boss, Operations Superintendent Ray Townsend.

Ray Townsend and friend: "Now I lay me down to sleep."

Ray, a World War II veteran, was an old-time "dirt-boot" forester, who had once mushed dog teams to cruise timber in the harsh winters of northern Quebec, where he had worked for the Canadian International Paper Company for twenty-five years. His outgoing and friendly personality, incessant (heh, heh) chuckle, questionable driving skills, shiny bald head, and voracious appetite for food presented us with a plethora of anecdotal fodder . . . more about him later!

Also in attendance at the staff meeting was Huntsville area supervisor Bill Brown, accountant Ross Williams and secretary Nancy LeBlanc, who was there to take minutes of the most interesting meeting I have ever attended.

It was time to act upon the vision.

During the introductions, we commented to each other about the fact that the four original AFA foresters sitting around the table were all graduates of the University of New Brunswick, each with extensive experience in the forest industry. No chance of failure here! There we were, in the early stages of the first Ontario government forestry authority ever established, and there wasn't a University of Toronto forester in sight. Joe would often be on the receiving end of friendly snipes about this from his U of T colleagues and friends. He reacted with a huge puff on his five-star Brigham pipe, with a billow of smoke hiding a couched smile, and a mumbled comment about an "objective process in search of value."

We were starting from scratch and needed everything from stubby pencils to half-ton trucks. For many years, I saved the minutes of that meeting to be referred to when required, as a reminder of how much we had accomplished over twenty-five years. They may still be in the AFA Pembroke office archives.

One of the first things that Joe and Ray did was to pull out a tattered old folded-up map of the park. It had been given to them to indicate operating areas scheduled for logging over the next three years under the previous regimes. There were no estimates of volumes or values. Talk about starting from a dead stop. We didn't even know how many jelly beans were in the jar, not to mention what colour they were.

But everybody knew what had to be done first. I can recall Ray offering with his usual chuckle, "You had better dust off the boots and find your tea pail, you are heading back into the bush, boys."

Bill Brown and I each rounded up a crew of timber cruisers and spent the next four months out in the park inventorying the forest. Once again, I found myself portaging canoes, cooking bacon over open fires, sleeping in tents, and casting for speckled trout in the evenings, just like thousands of canoe-trippers do each summer. Imagine! And some people aspire to be lawyers, accountants, and schoolteachers. Makes no sense to me!

Although we were spending most of our time in the bush during those early days, it was also necessary to visit and introduce ourselves to the mill owners and logging contractors with whom we would be doing business. This was the introductory phase of developing new relationships with the next cast of characters that would be forming a part of my life. Every day brought new excitement!

Heather remained in Sault Ste. Marie for most of that first summer waiting for the house to sell, while I camped out in the glory of Algonquin Park. It didn't seem to be fair, but what is a forester to do when called to duty? Finally, after two months our house sold, and we purchased an ideal home in Pembroke with six bedrooms located a "stone's throw" from the Civic Hospital. While looking for a small office to rent, I worked out of our home for a few weeks.

One afternoon I was working in the kitchen and had the table covered with maps and aerial photographs. I was looking at photographs through a stereoscope (an ocular device to produce three-dimensional images), when our daughter Janet approached and asked, "How are you making out, Dad?"

Looking up at her, I replied, "Not very well. I am trying to locate a road from out behind a huge swamp at Hogan Lake. I'm stuck and can't find a way out."

"You had better build a bridge or figure something else out soon," she said, "because Mom wants me to set the table for supper."

A one-room starter office was eventually rented near the bridge on the main street in Pembroke, and forester Bob Pick was hired as area forester. His first job was to gather and assemble forest inventory data and develop forest operational plans. Bob is a friendly, well-liked, bespectacled graduate of Lakehead University in Thunder Bay, Ontario. He is considered by many in the forestry profession as an expert in the management of white and red pine forests.

Bob and I worked closely together for twenty-five years. During that time, Bob's good nature and occasional little-boy innocence made him a natural subject for some wonderful stories. There are too many tales for the space available here, but I would like to share a few with you.

Bob Pick conducting a growth-and-yield demonstration for the AFA board of directors: "Going to have to drive this one a kick; it's not growing fast enough."

Brent A. Connelly

Bob and I teamed up on many occasions to do forest inventory and ground reconnaissance work in uncharted areas in Algonquin Park. The most memorable of our many trips together occurred one morning in late March in the Crooked Chute area near the Petawawa River. The snow was still deep, and with the warming March sun, it was necessary to take advantage of the early-morning crust. By noon it would be almost impossible to walk without sinking, even on snowshoes. We were out of the truck and on our snowshoes by 6:30 a.m. Bob was the compassman and led the way with a two-chain (132-foot) rope tied to the belt around his waist. I followed behind as the timber cruiser. We were frequently out of sight of each other.

It had snowed two inches the night before, and it hung in the branches of the spruce undergrowth, presenting a winter wonderland. The air was crisp and clear. There were no sounds or signs of wildlife, not even a whisky-jack following us in anticipation of a snack at lunchtime.

The silence could only be properly described by a poet. The wonder and magic of that morning was a spiritual experience, a million light years away from the madness of the Don Valley Parkway.

Around 11 o'clock, the sun began melting the snow in the branches, yielding a "swishing" sound as it fell gently to the ground. We were stopped, and Bob was ahead of me out of sight. With my head down, as I wrote in the tally book, I heard an unusual sound. I looked up to see a massive bull moose about twenty feet away, running directly towards me.

I had been motionless, so the moose didn't see me. But when I instinctively yelled at him, he immediately changed direction. The rope, which was tied to Bob's pants, became caught up in the moose's front leg as he ran. "What the hell are you doing back there?" Bob shouted with his arms around a tree, struggling to stay upright on his snowshoes.

Fortunately, the rope eventually fell away from the moose's leg, or Bob may have been skidded out to Opeongo Lake that morning—and we would still be looking for him! In 1995, Ray Townsend authored a book, *Algonquin Forestry Authority—A 20 Year History*. He included that story in the book.

Bob and I had another unique experience with wildlife, this time on a hot summer day in Fitzgerald Township. We were checking out an old logging road for the first time in an unfamiliar area. Bob was driving, and I had the aerial photographs on my knee to help guide us.

At one point we were not sure of our location. Bob stopped the truck and turned off the ignition. We both huddled over the photos, needing to confirm our position before continuing with the trip. The windows were wide open because of the heat, and as soon as Bob started the truck to leave, it must have startled a nearby partridge.

The frightened bird flew in through an open window and, in panic, bounced around the inside of the cab and behind the seat. It didn't take long for two wild-eyed foresters to bail out of the slow-moving truck. There we were, lying in the ditch spitting out feathers, as the truck and the partridge continued down the road for a short distance.

Only once in twenty-five years of working with Bob did I see him out of sorts. When Bob and I were setting up shop in Pembroke, we had the task of furnishing the one-room office. A list of our requirements was submitted to various suppliers for competitive quotations. The list included a light table, which was a vital item for foresters in those days before the arrival of Geographic Information Systems (GIS) technology.

A light table was one-foot high and approximately three-feet square. It came with a clear glass surface overtop florescent lights. It was used to trace detail from aerial photographs onto maps. Bob was working against a deadline in the preparation of an annual operating plan to be submitted to the Ministry of Natural Resources. He needed the light table to complete the map work. When placing the order, he noted "rush" on the light table. In a few days the order began to arrive in part—a chair one day and a filing cabinet the next—but still no sign of Bob's table.

After about two weeks Bob became anxious, and I overheard him on the phone pleading with the supplier for immediate delivery. One afternoon a few days later, I came in from the park to find Bob sitting at his desk. When he saw me, he covered his face and put his head down on the desk. It looked as if he had been sobbing.

"What's the matter, Bob?" I questioned.

"Can you believe that?" he shouted with frustration and pointed towards a corner of the office. There it was, a small wooden table about a foot square with four short legs, no more than a foot from the floor. It didn't have a glass surface or any florescent lights.

"There is my light table," Bob lamented. "The guy told me that he tried all over Canada and that is the lightest table he could find. Pembroke is going to be short one office equipment supplier when I get my hands on that son-of-bitch, and that's for sure."

"Don't fret, Bob," I said. "You may be able to use that little Barbie doll table as a foot stool when you finally get the real thing." The next morning when I came into the office, Bob was standing on a stepladder and had a map and some photographs taped to a window. He was tracing against the background of the early morning sunlight. "Don't need a frigging light table when you have a window," he grumbled.

Unusual things seemed to happen to Bob Pick! The Pick household was the subject of a neighbourhood watch campaign one time when he and his wife, Julie, adopted a big friendly Irish setter the size of a donkey and as dumb as a stump. The first trick that Kelly learned was to jump up on neighbours' cars and rip radio antennas off with her teeth and deposit them on Bob's back step. Kelly also began bringing home an array of implements such as shovels, rakes, and garden hoses. Efforts to tie the dog up with a logging chain failed.

Soon, Bob and Julie's backyard became a veritable garden centre and neighbours organized a vigilante movement. The last straw was the night that Kelly dragged home a twenty-pound propane tank from the barbeque next door. The following morning Bob transferred her to the safety of an Irish setter adoption agency.

Bob came in from the park one day missing the rear licence plate from his truck. In those days, it was not a simple matter to replace a licence plate. We had a government fleet arrangement, which took forever if replacement plates were needed. Bob decided that he was going to find his lost licence plate on his own and switched his front plate to the rear for the interim.

He put signs up at the park gate and sent out memos asking people to be on the lookout for his plate. Eventually, everybody travelling in the eastern regions of Algonquin Park was searching for Bob's missing plate, but without success. It was not found until over a year later when forest technician Peter VanderKraan came in from a day working in a remote area in Edgar Township.

"You're not going to believe this, Brent," he said. "I was driving on an old road overgrown with brush when I came across a clearing. It looked like an alien landing site or a blowdown area. Broken trees lying on the ground everywhere. I got out of my truck to investigate and discovered several deep tire ruts filled with stones and pieces of wood. Lying beside the ruts was a broken bumper jack, a shovel and, guess what? Bob's lost licence plate."

It wasn't difficult to imagine the events that had transpired. This was reluctantly confirmed by Bob when the long-lost plate was returned to him in front of as many onlookers as Peter and I could gather together at the time. Bob had been doing some reconnaissance by himself and got his truck stuck in a soft spot while turning around. We didn't have a mobile radio system at the time, so Bob couldn't call for help. It would have taken him several hours to walk out to a main road to flag down a ride.

He toiled all by himself for a couple of hours, jacking up the rear and filling the ruts with stones and chunks of wood to free the wheels. Finally, he had enough traction to get the truck moving.

Picture the scene. Bob with his head down, clenching the wheel with the grip of a NASCAR driver, his glasses crossways on his face, a dishevelled head of hair matted with mud, sweat, and dead blackflies, tires flinging a cloud of flying stones and debris behind the truck, and Bob not looking back, not even once. "Yes, sir," he thought, "I am getting the hell out of here. Have to get back to the office to see if my light table has been delivered yet."

Many years ago, Bob and I attended a Canadian Institute of Forestry meeting in the Centre Block of the Parliament Buildings in Ottawa. After the meeting had ended, we were walking out of the main entrance and noticed a lineup of people waiting to enter the House of Commons Gallery for Question Period. Neither one of us had attended Question Period before, so we decided to join the queue. And that is when the fun began!

As we approached the metal detector, I asked Bob if he had been through one of those electronic scanners before. He replied, "Nothing to it," and proceeded to give me a short course in the procedure. I went first and passed through without incident.

Bob followed directly behind me, and suddenly bells started ringing and lights flashing. Upon emptying his pockets, Bob was asked to set aside his four-inch Swiss Army knife. His Wild Bill Hickock belt buckle triggered the alarm on the second try, and as Bob passed through the third time, holding his pants up with one hand, the alarm went once again. This time, it was his steel-toed shoes.

"Yes, sir, nothing to it alright—if you are naked!"

Finally, my barefooted friend cleared the detector on his fourth attempt, only to be met by members of the parliamentary SWAT team. In an instant, they had him pinned and spread-eagled against a wall.

While I moved as far away from the scene as possible, a fellow next to me pondered, "I wonder who the hell that character is."

 "Never saw him before in my life," I replied, "but I sure hope they get the cuffs on him soon before they have to evacuate the Parliament Buildings."

During Question Period, the gallery was buzzing with Bob's grand entrance and most had little time to pay any attention to Lucien Bouchard's blather below.

True story? Absolutely! Embellished? Perhaps a little but, nevertheless, one of the best memories I have of the good times that Bob Pick and I shared over the years.

After the initial forest inventory blitz had been launched, it was time to get on with the business at hand of negotiating contracts with logging contractors and sales agreements with mill owners. It was vital that an uninterrupted flow of forest products be maintained to the various dependant mills.

The AFA was then, and remains today, a stand-alone, self-financed Crown agency. It had an arm's-length relationship with its parent, the Ontario Ministry of Natural Resources. The AFA general manager reported to a board of directors appointed by the government, and the chairman reported to the Minister of Natural Resources.

After some initial start-up funding from the government, the AFA became financially autonomous, recovering its production and administrative costs from the sale of forest products. Normal accounting and business practices were used, and the financial objective was to recover operating costs and provide the necessary capital investment for infrastructure improvements, such as roads and bridges.

Brent A. Connelly

Holy Old Whistlin'

For the first five years, the volumes supplied to the mills were based on previous consumption averages. As the forest inventory data became available, these allocation volumes were adjusted to reflect the capacity of the forest to grow and sustain that production. The adjustments resulted in lower volumes of high-quality sawlog and veneer log products—and an increased availability of lower-grade products, such as pulpwood and fuelwood.

In 1983, the original mandate to supply the mills with raw material was expanded to include the responsibility for forest management activity, such as tree marking, planting, and site-preparation operations. The package also included forest management planning and the maintenance of certain public access roads in the park.

The financing for this work was recovered by retaining a portion of the stumpage value (royalties payable to the government for the sale of Crown timber). The model established at that time was modified and adapted to eventually be applied to the production of forest products on Crown land throughout the province.

Meanwhile, the tempo of field activity increased, and Bob hired a small crew of cruisers and tree markers. I was involved in talking to logging contractors who had previously been employed by the former timber licence holders. They would now be working directly for the AFA.

One Friday afternoon shortly after the moose incident with Bob, I was working at my desk and looked up to see a tall, slender, good-looking young fellow standing in the doorway. He had his résumé in an envelope and handed it to me, asking quietly, "Do you have any work for a good man?"

His name was Danny Janke, and he was graduating from the Forestry Technician Program at Algonquin College in Pembroke that spring. I interviewed him and was impressed, but had to advise that there was nothing available at that time. I explained that Bob already had a crew working, but would give his résumé to him in case the situation changed.

"Thank you," he said, "I'll be back." And he did come back—the next Friday, and the week after that, and the next one after that. He came back every week for the next couple of months. The man was wearing a path from the college to our office. His visits were brief, and he only stayed long enough to ask, politely, "Anything turn up, yet?"

Finally, I said to Bob, "Whenever you need someone, hire that guy, even if it is only for a day. I'm seeing him in my sleep." What a great example of determination he was! Something any young person looking for employment should emulate.

Danny became a regular employee a few months later and worked for us for several years as a logging supervisor. He went on to obtain his MBA at the University of Ottawa in the mid 1990s, and I am proud to say succeeded me as AFA's operations manager in Pembroke in 1999.

Danny Janke was the man behind the classic quote made by a wood-processing contractor to logging-equipment dealer Harry Searson of Eganville. We had hired the contractor for a two-week period to process tree lengths into log products in a Pembroke millyard. Danny was his direct supervisor working against a tight production deadline.

When the project was finished, the contractor stopped at Harry's shop to have some repairs done to his equipment. As they chatted about the newly formed AFA, the contractor explained that he had done well on the job and, with an approving chuckle, added, "The AFA rented a hotel room for me to stay in and that young lad, Danny Janke, had me working until ten o'clock each night. He was banging on my door at five o'clock in the morning ready to start the next shift. They didn't need to rent me a room at all. I could have got by with a blanket on a frigging chair and a footstool in the lobby."

Our humble little office in Pembroke needed a secretary to help with the increased activity, so I advertised the job in the local papers and set up a day to interview six candidates. An hour and a half was allocated for each interview, but unfortunately the schedule overlooked one very important detail. People who attend job interviews usually arrive well before the specified time.

Such was the case with Genda Scott who, on a very cold, rainy day, opened the front door of the one-room office with an umbrella in hand to find me in the midst of an interview with another candidate. What to do? It was an awkward moment. I had to think fast.

There was no place for her to wait, so after the initial moment of panic, I gave her the keys to my truck outside. I asked her if she would mind waiting there until I had finished. She agreed cheerfully, tossed it off with a smile and climbed into the truck as I desperately tried to brush the traces of mud from the seat and tuck my boots and a chunk of chain behind the seat. Genda had the qualifications for the job and, along with her good-natured reaction to the stress of the moment, it was not difficult to decide upon her as the successful candidate.

As I was mopping up late that afternoon before going home, the phone rang. I answered to hear a message, which I had often anxiously anticipated in one form or another. It echoed of the warnings that I had received from friends at Weyerhaeuser in Sault Ste. Marie, when they chided me, "What the hell are you doing quitting a perfectly good job here to jump into a black hole like Algonquin Park? The AFA will be as brief as the flick of a firefly. The environmentalists will tear you apart; you will be back with us before the sap runs in the spring."

The caller had a muffled European accent and was obviously talking into a conference phone. He introduced himself as Dr. Von Oostrom, the executive director of the Algonquin Wildlands League.

"Mr. Connelly," he snarled, "last night we had a meeting of our Ottawa chapter and were outraged to receive a report that your organization has an active logging operation causing major damage to the nesting trees in a unique, protected habitat of the endangered purple-breasted falk-bird. I have been trying all day, unsuccessfully, to reach the Minster of Natural Resources to insist on a moratorium of your operations, but I will certainly be talking to him tomorrow. In the meantime, I am calling you to demand that you stop this insanity immediately and shut the operation down tonight before it resumes tomorrow morning."

By this time he had my full attention! I had already reached for a pad and pen and was scrambling to take notes. I had always enjoyed observing birds when travelling in the bush (something that came from my time with "Hay Lake" Joe); however, I had never heard of the purple-breasted falk-bird. I realized instantly that this was serious, and I would need as much information as possible, so I began asking some questions.

His knowledge of the life pattern of the bird was extensive and impressive. It apparently overwintered in a localized area north of Biloxi, Mississippi, and migrated to the same nesting areas in Algonquin Park each year. It had been doing this for many generations. The bird was the same size as a bluebird, had a deep purple breast, light blue wing tips, and a yellow beak. A designer bird to be sure—it sounded beautiful. I was beginning to feel sick.

I had a page full of notes, but still did not know the location of the problem. I asked him what township the nesting area was in as I stood up to look at a map on the wall. "We are not sure of the township," he replied, "but it is an operation that you have about one half a mile northeast of the inlet into Splashy Lake." I had not heard of Splashy Lake and couldn't find it on the map after a quick glance. I mentally put that small detail aside to follow up on later. Finally, I had all the information that I thought would be necessary, including his phone number. I promised him a return call after looking into the situation.

But before hanging up, I wanted to ensure that I had the correct spelling of the bird.

"Is the name of the bird spelled f-a-l-k ?"

"No, no, no," he interrupted. "It's f-u-c-k bird. Have you never heard of the purple-breasted fuck-bird, you stupid son-of-a-bitch? Algonquin Park is doomed now. What kind of a forest manager are you, anyway?"

As I picked myself up off the floor, I heard a loud roar of background laughter from the other end of the phone. It was a rollicking Tony Vorlicek, my old boss and good friend from Weyerhaeuser days. He asked in his normal voice, "And what kind of a day are you having down in Algonquin Park today, Brent? Are you walking the fine line yet?" Tony had rounded up a few of the boys around the conference phone in the boardroom for the performance. He may even have charged admission!

"The timber in the area that you want me to cut is so scattered, the woodpeckers have to pack a lunch or they will starve, just like I will, if I sign your goddamned logging contract."
—Walter Dombroski, logging contractor

Most of the logging contractors I did business with over the years stood tall in my eyes. They were special people. Like farmers, they were hard-working, fiercely proud, and stubbornly independent. They constantly worked on the precipice of risk, facing the variables of weather, terrain and, at times, a persnickety marketplace.

Walter Dombroski from Barry's Bay was one such individual. A robust man of average height in his mid forties at the time, he boasted a larger-than-life red moustache. His square profile and abundant waist often sported three or four inches of dangling leather belt, which seemed to be searching for the safety of the next belt loop.

Walter was proud of his Polish ancestry and his success as a major logging contractor, having started from very humble beginnings. He talked at the speed of light, and it took me several months to catch on to his staccato-like dialogue, only to discover that everything he said made sense. The exception was when it came time to sign him to a logging contract. At that time, it was necessary to closely examine the doomsday rhetoric, which he presented in a skilled and dramatic fashion.

Of all the men that I have ever known, Walter Dombroski was one of the most multi-skilled and intelligent. He possessed the memory of a herd of elephants. The man could do everything from operating or repairing any piece of equipment mounted on wheels or tracks, to making the best garlic dill pickles and smoked sausage known to man.

In addition to being a logger, he was a plumber, an electrician, a mechanic, a carpenter, a cook, a butcher, a cattleman, a fish farmer, a municipal politician, a maple syrup producer—the list is endless. One day as I was marvelling at all his talents, he explained that he had to leave school at a very early age to help raise a large family. His father, consequently, taught him to never miss an opportunity to watch others at work and not be shy to ask questions. "That is how I learned," he said. "When I was a boy, my education was out in the bush, in the hay field, or garage, or even the kitchen paying attention to men and women at work." As a young boy, he frequently tagged along with his father picking up scrap metal and wood, which was frequently crafted into something useful and often marketable. I am convinced that the only reason that Walter can't fly a jumbo jet or play a harp today is that nobody ever showed him how.

Aside from the normal annual logging contracts, we frequently hired Walter and his crew to construct or move logging camps. In one case, he presided over a celebratory barbeque we had arranged at an historic site at Basin Depot in Algonquin Park. The event commemorated the restoration of a heritage cabin, which Walter and his men had completed for us.

Brent A. Connelly

Holy Old Whistlin'

81

The menu was Polish roast pig with all the trimmings. Walter showed up the night before with an ample supply of Crown Royal and a barbeque spit that he had made himself. The spit would have made an MIT engineer drool with envy. He had combined the remnants of an old cream separator with a transmission salvaged from the carcass of a Ford half-ton truck, along with an assortment of belts and pulleys.

It had an equal number of forward and reverse gears and a "what-the-hell-is-that-thing" look to it. After a night of roasting with generous applications of his secret Kazuby basting sauce, Walter presented us with an outstanding tasty treat that Emeril Lagasse couldn't touch with a ten-foot pole.

In the early stages of the business relationship with Walter, I arranged for Joe Bird and Ray Townsend to come over to meet him. We planned on him becoming one of our regular contractors. It was an evening meeting held at Walter's logging camp at Stewart's Spur in the eastern region of the park.

After a delicious supper of roast beef, cabbage, and potatoes, we retired to Walter's office—a modest lumber structure about twelve-feet square with a crooked stovepipe sticking out one end. The building stood alone at one end of the camp yard. So, against the background of an early evening darkness on a cool November night, Walter opened the door for us to enter. What a completely amazing sight it was, one that Joe, Ray, and I have described to unbelieving audiences on many occasions since.

Along one wall was a small table sitting beside a wooden CIL dynamite box in a corner. Three rickety, wooden chairs leaned up against the walls in the other corners. On the table was a one-armed mechanical adding machine, a tackle box, and a huge pickle jar filled with an assortment of stubby pencils, paper clips, chainsaw files, and spark plugs. A battered filing cabinet beside the table looked as if it had fallen off a truck. It probably had! A huge outdated Racquel Welch calendar was spiked to a wall.

It was what was in the middle of the room that stopped us all in our tracks, making this the most unusual boardroom meeting that any of us had ever attended. The room's centrepiece was a dead fox hanging from the ceiling by its tail—its nose about four feet from the floor and dripping blood into a pail.

Walter went on to tell us that on his drive in from the bush that afternoon, the fox darted in front of his truck. He couldn't avoid hitting him and stopped to see if he could help the animal. But its injuries were fatal. "Couldn't put a splint on the poor little bugger so here he is. Can't waste a good fox pelt," he explained.

As I came to know Walter better in later years I saw glimpses of his sometimes masked compassion for all life. I am convinced that if the fox could have been helped, Walter would have done so—probably with skills acquired from watching an old veterinarian someplace.

The meeting commenced with Walter sitting on the box and the others teetering precariously on the old chairs. After a few minutes, the distraction caused by the occasional drip of blood into the pail diminished. We quickly caught on to maintaining eye contact with each other by peeking around the dripping remains of Walter's trophy.

I will never forget my attendance at that "four men and a fox summit," as we discussed the future of logging in Algonquin Park. The anti-logging faction would have had a field day with that picture.

"If you are going to be successful negotiating a contract with a logging contractor, you had better do your homework—right down to the cost of 'axe handles' and 'pork hocks.'"
—I.D. (Joe) Bird, AFA general manager

Modern-day management consultants make a great deal of money delivering courses on the principles of negotiation. None of these experts has ever met a case study quite like Walter Dombroski.

Walter contracted for a number of years with Johnnie Shaw to produce logs for Shaw Lumber in Pembroke. The only contract involved in this relationship was a firm handshake and a few numbers scrawled on a cigarette package attached to the back of the sun visor of a half-ton truck—filed along with a stack of parts orders, maps, invoices, Kentucky Fried Chicken coupons, and speeding tickets.

Then along came the AFA with its multi-page contract of "save harmless and performance" legalese, product specifications, f.o.b. rates, and delivery schedules. When I first introduced the document to Walter, he almost fainted and then growled, "I have six truck drivers working for me. Looks like I will have to hire more frigging lawyers than that to get a job with you fellows."

To complete the first contract with him, it took a couple of marathon sessions to establish rates and clarify some of the terms and conditions before an agreement was eventually reached. Finally, I had a contract for Walter to sign, which I delivered in person to his garage. As he flipped up the face of the welding mask he was wearing, he placed the contract on a nearby anvil and initialled each page with a WD, while inadvertently leaving a trail of black thumb prints on a number of pages.

Walter's normal negotiating strategy, backed up with well researched preparation, was to show up without a pencil or pad. He would take a chair and sit back with his arms wrapped around his huge midriff and state flatly, "I need a ten per cent increase over what you paid me last year. All I am doing in the logging business these days is trading dollars for pennies, and I'm not the one getting the dollars. The only thing I got from last year's job was a sore back and a grease pail full of rusty frigging pennies."

It was as predictable as Jack McRae's rants, and we would start from there. Committed to memory, Walter would deliver an accurate, verbatim account of the latest increase in the OPEC price of world crude oil and the increased cost of buying and operating logging equipment. I could also expect an update on his obligations ranging from truck licences to UIC and OHIP contributions.

One spring day, I visited his office in Barry's Bay to begin negotiations on a contract for the upcoming year. I brought along a newly acquired laptop computer. It was fully loaded with a spreadsheet detailing a logging appraisal summarizing an estimate of my version of the contractor's costs, right down to the cost of a side of beef for the cookery.

I had impressed myself by the enormous amount of information that I had available at the touch of a key and thought, "Boy, I am going to dazzle that old bugger this time."

Walter glanced at me and, with a twitch of his bushy moustache, grinned and said, "Just when I thought I had you figured out, Brent, you have gone all to hell carrying your brains around in a goddamned packsack." And while pointing to his head with a forefinger nicked and bruised from fighting slipped wrenches, he added, "I carry mine between my ears—can't lose them that way."

Walter and I had some intense negotiation sessions over the years. There were instances of us stomping out on each other on a few occasions, but always prepared to reconvene in a few days. Perhaps there would be a little story to begin the next session. Of course, there was always some new information intending to influence and soften the other's position.

The bottom line, however, is that when a contract was signed with Walter Dombroski, the wood was produced and delivered within budget, as stipulated. Not once in twenty-five years did he ever let me down. In recent years he has moved to the background, turning the day-to-day operation of the logging business over to his three sons, Larry, Nicky, and Joey, who demonstrate that they have learned well at the knee of a real master.

The subject of negotiations takes us briefly back to Weyerhaeuser and a learning experience that I had with the mayor of Elliot Lake. Weyerhaeuser held a licence to harvest timber on Crown land surrounding the new town site of Elliot Lake. In the late sixties, when I was working for the company, the town was booming and growing very rapidly. The development of the town was presided over by a government-appointed administrative manager. He was not elected, but was still referred to by everyone in town as "The Mayor."

The town had been hacked right out of the bush, and one of the many things they needed to do first was construct a cemetery. There were some control problems, as would be expected, but in their zeal to get the job done, they had a bulldozer flatten about fifteen acres of Crown land containing prime hardwood timber. No attempt was made to seek approval or salvage the valuable timber. Lotars Kakis, one of our foresters, made the discovery accidentally when he was in the area timber cruising.

Had we been contacted beforehand, it would have been a straightforward matter to accommodate their requirements.

To make matters worse, the Ontario Department of Lands and Forests held us, as the licensee, responsible for any unauthorized cutting or trespasses on the licenced area. They were going to fine us, so the least I had to do was recover this amount and the value of the lost timber. We decided to go beyond that and impose an additional penalty to drive home the seriousness of the incident. I was going to Elliot Lake to demand a substantial compensation package.

I called the mayor to arrange a meeting and made it quite clear I had to see him. The next day I arrived at his office. It was a large office, even larger than Mansiel Wilson's, and the walls were covered with hunting and fishing trophies. The mayor was a huge, middle-aged, pot-bellied man with a beaming smile and a friendly face. He sat in a big, high-topped leather chair behind an oval desk the size of a pool table.

After we shook hands and I sat down, he immediately started to apologize for the inconvenience that had been caused. He explained in a very serious tone that people were already starting to die in town—he had to act quickly! He poured me a cup of coffee and passed me some chocolate-coated doughnuts. He had done his homework and was ready for me.

However, I wasn't going let him off the hook and went right after him, like a pitbull. I had my arguments well thought out and figured I had the momentum at that point. I even went as far as mentioning that legal proceedings were quite common in situations like this.

When I told him what we required for compensation, he looked shocked, sat back in his chair, and fell silent. It looked as if he were going to weep! He finally countered with an outrageously low amount. I declined, and he went silent on me again.

Then I made my mistake. On his desk directly in front of me was something unusual, which caught my eye. It was a strange, thin, stick-like object about six inches long, mounted vertically on a clear plastic base. While he sat there silently in an attempt to outwait me, I foolishly asked what the object was. His eyes lit up and he replied, "It's the penis of a bear that I shot last year up on the White River."

I couldn't have fallen into that hole any better if I had dug it myself. From there, he led me on a marathon of stories about his various hunting expeditions. He pulled out photo albums and held me spellbound for about a half hour. When he had finished, it was as if we had become fast friends. I thought he was going to ask me to go fishing with him in the spring.

I had completely lost my train of thought and certainly my momentum. He had introduced me to the commonly used diversionary tactic used by good negotiators. After the dust had settled, we sawed off at a compromised amount that was well below my initial position. I had recovered our out-of-pocket losses, but drew a blank with most of the punitive component.

As I drove home that night I couldn't help but think, "That old bugger outfoxed me with a bear's prick—another lesson learned." I have used the same tactic many times over the years and found that sometimes it was necessary and helpful to take the other party on "a trip around the world" before the timing was right to return to the area of disagreement.

"The Friendly Giant of Mattawa," logging contractor Ed Wunsch, was also a master at this technique. Ed, a huge soft-spoken and good-natured man, was well known in the forestry business as an excellent logging contractor. He was also well respected in his community of Mattawa for his benevolence towards friends and residents troubled by illness or other misfortune. He had many friends.

I was in Ed's office in Calvin Township one day negotiating logging contract rates for the upcoming season. His position centred around rising fuel costs and other increases to his operating costs. My story was that the mills were suffering from poor sales due to a slow economy. That year, we were unable to provide anything more than slight nominal adjustments.

Ed never put a number on the table. He sat back with his big grin and let me propose the rates and then react with a grunt indicating, "Not good enough." On this particular day, we were making fair progress until we hit a snag on a couple of items. At that point, I accelerated my position with fresh arguments supported by some sophisticated economic indicators that I had brought along (my briefcase was stuffed with copies of the *Financial Post* and the *Wall Street Journal*).

I was gaining momentum, or so I thought.

Ed didn't react. Instead, he left his chair and went over to the window to look out over a pond, which he had made to host flocks of migrating Canada geese. "Well, I'll be a son-of-a-bitch," he said. "You are not going to believe this, Brent, come and have a look. There is an albino goose in the pond with my geese. That's a first. I'll have to go over and see if he will come to me—as soon as you get the log rates right."

Once again, we were off on another "winged migration roundabout," completely unrelated to the subject at hand. Ed was an expert on geese and could go on indefinitely about their habits. My momentum evaporated before my eyes. I had been foiled one more time!

I will close off this part by offering some hard-earned advice to any prospective managers and negotiators who may be browsing: In the event that you find yourself in a corner during negotiations, make sure that you have a bear's penis handy and an old albino goose tied up out back somewhere.

"Odenback Depot calling Pembroke Base: It's been a long winter, the men are getting 'frisky' and they want to go home to their wives. Flag down the next log truck you see and send me up a case of 'salt peter' [sexual inhibitor]."
—Richard (Dick) Shalla, logging superintendent, Odenback Depot, Algonquin Park

In the early years, the absence of a universal mobile radio system in Algonquin Park was a major concern as well as an inconvenience for everybody involved in logging operations. The dispatch of ambulances to logging accidents was occasionally delayed or, in some cases, misdirected because of this lack of communication. Routine business was often left for phone calls from home in the evenings.

Therefore, one of the first major investments the AFA initiated was a radio system consisting of tower linkages and truck and base-unit installations. This enabled contractors and AFA personnel to talk to each other from most areas. Emerging technological advances eventually led to independent systems. But for the first few years, one could overhear all radio communications among contractors, their crews, and AFA personnel and office base stations.

At times, there was great entertainment value to this feature. One particular incident comes to mind involving Walter Dombroski who, when excited, could resemble a runaway Gatling gun. BRRRRRRRrrrrrr!!!

I had stayed overnight at Walter's Stewart's Spur camp one night. At breakfast the next morning, I overheard Walter and his foreman, John Jeffreys, planning the day ahead of them. They were in the process of moving the log-hauling operation from one location to another, and John was to escort the loader and operator to the new loading site. Walter planned to meet the empty trucks and lead them to the loader's new location.

"I'll meet you 'up over the big hill' at eight o'clock, John," Walter said as he climbed into his truck.

Later on that morning at a few minutes to eight as I was driving to Odenback Depot, the site of another logging camp operated by Canada Veneers Ltd., I heard Walter on the radio, "Dombroski One to Dombroski Four, do you have a copy, John?"

"Go ahead, Walter," John replied.

"Where are you now?" Walter asked.

"I am 'up over the big hill' waiting for you," John answered.

Sounding puzzled, Walter came back saying, "I am 'up over the big hill,' too, and I don't see you anywhere, John."

Walter Dombroski: "What 'up over the big hill' are you at, John?"

There was an extended pause and in a few minutes Walter came on again, "Dombroski One to Dombroski Four, what 'up over the big hill' are you at, John?"

"I am 'up over the big hill' south of McNorton Lake."

"Holy shit, John," Walter groaned. "You are at the wrong 'up over the big hill.' I'm 'up over the big hill' near the swamp where you and I saw the two moose last week."

Once again I had to stop my truck until I could stop laughing. Abbott and Costello's "Who's on first, What's on second?" skit will never be a match for that gem.

He who laughs at another as I did that day should always expect to have the favour returned. The one time it happened to me, it was Walter who was slapping his knees.

The AFA, the Ministry of Natural Resources, Pembroke Algonquin College Forestry Faculty, and the former Forest Products Accident Prevention Association were collaborating on a training video illustrating safe and efficient logging practices. Several of the people involved in the project, including the film crew and Walter with some of his men, had gathered on a log landing one day. Some tree-felling and log-skidding action was scheduled for filming. The whole group (probably ten people) was standing not far from my truck, discussing what was to take place next.

It was in the summer, and the windows of my truck were wide open. Everybody on site and throughout Algonquin Park who was within radio range could overhear the clear female voice on my radio. This in itself was unusual, as regular communication was by far male dominated.

"Algonquin Four from Sweetheart One?" was the salutation, which could be heard by everybody in North America. I was stunned and hesitated for a minute, not knowing quite what to do. It was Heather's voice and I realized that she was in our Pembroke office. She was taking the opportunity to set me up.

"You had better answer your radio, Brent," Walter grinned, "Sounds important to me."

Timidly, I picked up the mike and whispered, "Go ahead."

This was followed by the question, "Will you be home at the regular time for supper tonight, darling?"

"Yes," was my meek reply. "Algonquin Four clear."

"See you then. Sweetheart One clear," and Heather signed off.

Later that evening as we chuckled over the incident, I said to her, "I could kick myself for not thinking of it until I was driving home. I should have said to you, 'Sweetheart One, is that you, Heather?' That would have fixed you!" To this day, whenever I meet Peter VanderKraan he always asks with a huge laugh, "And how is Sweetheart One these days?" It was a keeper for him!

There is an unwritten "code of the bush," which is contained in the loggers' constitution. If you ever get your truck stuck on a bush road, under no circumstances must anyone else find out about it— never, never, never. Especially over the radio.

There are only three choices to consider: work like a mule by yourself to jack or lever the truck free; walk to town for as long as it takes and hire a wrecker to come out in the middle of the night to pull the truck out; or wait until your bones are found.

However, some could become quite creative in calling for help over the community radio system without revealing they were actually stuck. I was travelling in the Achray area one morning when I overheard a call from Bob Pick to Dave Barras, "Algonquin Five to Algonquin Seven."

"Go ahead, Bob," Dave replied.

"Dave, I'm over on the Lone Creek Road locating a new branch road and there is a creek here that you should see. Can you come over and do a stream-flow analysis for me?"

"Sure thing, Bob," Dave replied. "I am not far from there and will be right over." And that was that.

However, about two hours later, Dave came on the radio calling Danny Janke, "Algonquin Seven to Algonquin One. What is your location, Danny?"

"I'm on the Achray Road not too far from Lone Creek," was Danny's reply.

Brent A. Connelly

Holy Old Whistlin'

Dave responded, "Bob and I are on the Lone Creek Road laying out a branch road with a tricky side cut on it. We are wondering if you could stop by to give us a third opinion."

"Will be there in twenty minutes, Dave," replied Danny.

Instantly, I knew this was not as it appeared to be. These guys were all independent thinkers and not given to forming committees unnecessarily. I didn't hear any further calls that day and suspected that the problem had been fixed.

I was curious to find out the rest of the story, however, and my opportunity came the following Friday afternoon at a staff meeting. After a particularly gruelling part of the meeting, I decided to lighten it up a bit and asked Bob, Dave, and Danny how they made out with that "tricky side cut" at Lone Creek the other day.

Their quick glances to each other and tiny smiles told the real story, but their response was both united and low-key. "No problem. We spread out on the hill and were able to come up with a good line of sight and alignment. Good thing there were three of us; it made the job easier. The log trucks won't have any problems there."

This wasn't any fun, so I persisted. "You guys can't bullshit me. You were stuck weren't you?" Eventually, they confessed. They were not good at telling lies.

Bob was the first to get stuck in a mud hole. Dave came to his rescue and also became stuck. Finally Danny, the last of my "Three Stooges," came to meet his fate in the same mud hole, while trying to pull out the other two trucks. The scene: a parade of mud-splattered cowboys, stranded, scratching their heads, and going nowhere. The story ended with them walking a couple of miles to fetch a skidder from Gordon Stewart's operation to pull them all out.

I added insult to their injury. "I can't believe you guys—you should have called me to come over and pull you all out with my mighty Ford Ranger. Your secret would have been safe with me."

Glen Hamilton is a prince of a guy. He was our senior log scaler and had worked for the Ministry of Natural Resources for many years before joining the AFA. He was in his early fifties as I approached retirement. His closely cropped black hair, which didn't contain a trace of grey, and his handsomely boyish face caused him to be often mistaken for a man in his thirties.

Glen was a soft-spoken person, possessing a keen sense of humour and good-natured outlook on life. Unlike many of his colleagues in the forest industry, he seldom used profanity. He was well liked and respected by all who worked with him. He took his work very seriously, consistently showing up for work well before starting time. As neat as a pin, his AFA truck was always shined on the outside and vacuumed on the inside, as if it had come directly from the showroom. Glen was in a class by himself, organized right down to his last pencil and the next log pile to be measured.

Up until the early 1980s, the Ministry of Natural Resources operated a work centre at Achray Station on Grand Lake in the eastern region of Algonquin Park. The centre was at the same site as an historical cabin once used by legendary artist Tom Thomson. The scene of his *Jack Pine* painting was situated directly across the lake at Carcajou Bay.

AFA Pembroke staff and MNR staff at Achray worked closely with each other and frequently held joint meetings at Achray. The meetings were usually held in the evenings to allow participants to drive there at the end of the day from their various work sites.

On one such occasion, several of us from the AFA arrived in our own vehicles from different locations in time for supper in the cookery. Attending the meeting was logging foreman Percy Bresnahan, who had grown up with Glen in Madawaska, Ontario. He was a renowned practical joker and could never resist an opportunity.

Dave Millard told me that he was once walking in the bush with Bresnahan on an extremely hot summer day. Dave was in the lead and after they had puffed their way to the top of a steep hill, Dave stopped for a breather. He looked back and, in amazement, saw Percy carrying a huge stone, the sweat flying off his face and his knees buckling under its load. "Here, Dave," Percy offered, "you take this for awhile. It's too hot to carry it another step."

After our meeting was over that night a few of us were walking through the parking lot to the bunkhouse. Percy spotted Glen's truck and turned to me and said, "How about playing a little trick on Glen?"

"Not a chance," I replied. "I don't want to be any part of embarrassing Glen."

That was Percy's cue to proceed. He opened the door of Glen's truck and disconnected the mike and cord from his mobile radio and hid it behind the seat. I could see it all unfolding before me.

The next morning, we left at different times to our various destinations for the day. Shortly after I was underway, I overheard Percy calling on the radio, "Algonquin One to Algonquin Three, do you have a copy, Glen?" No answer.

I could clearly see poor old Glen driving along the Lake Travers Road, hearing the call, and reaching down for his mike to respond to find out that he didn't have a mike. A few minutes went by and then another call, still no answer.

The next call was to me. "Algonquin One to Algonquin Four. Brent, did you see Glen this morning?"

"Yes, Percy," I said. "I saw him at breakfast. He must have left for work before any of the rest of us."

"I don't think so," Percy replied. "I can't reach him on the radio. He must have gone back to bed after breakfast. That's the second time this week the little bugger has been late for work. What the hell are we going to do about that guy?"

A few minutes later as I drove around a curve on the Lake Travers Road, I saw Glen's truck in the ditch. He was standing nearby kicking a tree. I stopped, and as I approached, he asked, "Can I have the afternoon off? I have to go to Pembroke to the army surplus store to buy a gun. I am going to shoot that son-of-a-gun of a Bresnahan, that potlucker!"

For a few minutes that morning Glen and I shared a good laugh and then went cheerfully on about our business.

"Did you the hear the story about the 'tea-pail-twit from Toronto'?"
—Unknown Algonquin Park forest firefighter

I caught up to Glen that morning of the malfunctioning mike near the Barron Canyon Lookout parking lot. The recollection now triggers a fit of masochistic compulsion to relate my Barron Canyon story. It's confession time once again, as I take this opportunity to laugh at myself, doing so at great personal risk.

Once, I had the opportunity to roast a former mayor of Pembroke, Les Scott, at a celebrity charity event. He reciprocated with this story, complete with a bag full of props. My secret had escaped!

The beautiful Barron River flows through the eastern regions of Algonquin Park before entering the Petawawa River and eventually the Ottawa River at Petawawa. It has everything one could dream of: still waters, tumbling rapids, and spectacular falls. Ten thousand years ago, a receeding glacier drained the former Lake Algonquin, which was the forerunner of the Upper Great Lakes. The Friends of Algonquin Barron Canyon Trail Guide notes that a geologist once suggested that "at its peak ten thousand years ago the river must have carried as much water as a thousand Niagara Falls."

The centrepiece of the river is a canyon less than an hour's drive from Pembroke. And overlooking the canyon is a viewing area accessible by a 1.5-kilometre hiking trail loop maintained by Ontario Parks. From the lookout, one can marvel at a 300-foot, rock-faced chasm rising up from the gently flowing river below.

This site is breathtaking. Fortunately, due to the wisdom of such fine park superintendents as John Winters, Ernie Martelle and others before them, the site has been preserved in its natural state. There are no vending telescopes or souvenir shops, although clearly visible signage warns visitors of the need to control children while walking along the edge of the canyon.

Several times over the years, our family enjoyed canoeing on the river and camping at the Achray campsite on Grand Lake. On one occasion, the men of the family formed a party of four canoes consisting of my three sons, who were barely teenagers at the time; my brothers-in law, Ken MacTavish and Jack Lavis; and their sons Neil and John.

We planned to paddle down the river from Grand Lake to a take-out point at the bridge near the park gate on the Lake Travers Road. We were to camp overnight for two nights at campsites along the river. It was a hot Victoria Day long weekend, and the forest fire hazard was very high. We were warned at the park gate to take extreme caution and that fires were for cooking purposes only.

It was a thrilling experience: canoeing, swimming, and visiting High Falls where the boys frolicked under the sparkling water for a couple of hours. Talk about your male bonding experience. Not a sister or a wife in sight, and we didn't even notice.

On the last afternoon of the trip, while paddling about a mile upstream from the Barron Canyon, we caught the distinctive whiff of a forest fire. As we rounded the turn in the river and approached the canyon at a point directly below the lookout, we saw smoke wisping away from the canyon wall. It was obvious that this was a dangerous situation and that quick action was necessary.

I was in the stern of the lead canoe, and in my role as the trip's chief guide, I immediately led the wide-eyed members of the party to shore. A small tea pail was retrieved from my packsack and filled with water. I then proceeded to climb up over the huge boulders which lay at the bottom of the canyon. The footing was poor, and each time I stepped from one boulder to another, a little water would spill from the pail.

From river level looking up the wall of the canyon, it was difficult to judge the extent of the fire. After climbing up about forty feet, it became apparent that the moss carpeting the canyon wall was smouldering. The whole face of the canyon was on fire. I realized that there was nothing that I could do to help with the small amount of water left in the tiny tea pail. In frustration, I threw the remaining cupful on a nearby hot spot.

At that instant, I was greeted by the roar of a massive cheer and applause from the lookout area above. I glanced up to see about forty MNR firefighters in their bright orange coveralls and hard hats peeking out over the edge of the canyon. They were clapping and hooting like a bunch of damned fools, cheering me on.

I learned later that they had been fighting the fire all weekend with fire pumps and even a helicopter. It was not one of my finer moments.

Fortunately, I was not recognized. I was wearing sunglasses and was able to pull my hat down over my ears as soon as the cheering began. As I scrambled back to the canoe to join my howling

Brent A. Connelly

Holy Old Whistlin'

companions, I declared confidently, "We might as well keep on going—looks like these boys have the situation pretty much in hand."

Later that evening at home, as the rest of the family was being told about the experience (not by me, but by others), our son Michael jokingly asked, "Dad, would it hurt your feelings if I had my last name changed?"

A few weeks after the incident, I was in the MNR Achray office on business. Several of the same firefighters were there enjoying themselves, laughing about the incident. They weren't aware that it was me they were laughing about.

In the midst of all the fun, my old friend Roger Mask, who was not there the afternoon of the fire, remarked, "Sure would like to meet that stupid son-of-a-bitch. He must be from Toronto—couldn't find his arse with two hands, naked in broad daylight."

I had not laughed much to that point, but decided to chip in anyway saying, "Maybe you have met him, Roger. He has probably stayed here at your Achray campsite. And, yes I agree, he was more than likely from Toronto or Southern Ontario someplace. Dummies like that don't come from the Ottawa Valley."

So now you know, Roger. You did meet that stupid son-of-a-bitch, many times in fact. The last time was a chance meeting and storytelling interlude near the food court in the Pembroke Mall. Now, don't you be telling anybody.

Roger Mask worked in Algonquin Park for the Ontario Department of Lands and Forests, Ministry of Natural Resources, and Ontario Parks for most of his career. He knew Algonquin Park like the back of his hand, always taking a keen interest in the people who worked and relaxed there. He could spin a yarn about some of these characters with the best of them.

You knew that a treat was on its way when you found Roger sitting back in a chair, occasionally stroking his bushy Mansiel-Wilson-like eyebrows, with his legs crossed and a match in hand, ready to light up the old pipe.

He had me in stitches once, describing a sight he experienced while working in his office in the "old stone building" on the shore of Grand Lake at Achray. Again, it was a very hot and humid summer day. The air was still without the slightest trace of a breeze. About two in the afternoon, Roger noticed a strong wind coming across the lake. A huge threatening black cloud moved quickly in a southeasterly direction over the hill at Carcajou Bay.

He stepped out onto the verandah overlooking the beach to watch the incoming storm and noticed an aluminum rowboat out in the middle of the lake. The only occupant was an old, shirtless, bald-headed guy with a fishing rod in his hand. Roger went on to describe what happened next.

"The wind became quite severe, and then along came a few hailstones the size of golf balls. From where I was, I could hear the pinging sounds as they hit the bottom of the boat. At first, the old lad tried to protect his bald head with his hands, but then a huge sheet of hailstones came his way. He jammed a small pail over his head, grabbed the oars, and rowed like hell towards shore.

"As he approached shore, I could see the welts starting to appear on his back. The hailstones bounced off the tin pail and rolled around in the bottom of the boat—sounded like Spike Jones' Band, and I'm sure the racket could be heard in Pembroke. When he finally beached his boat, he bolted to the office for shelter. The poor old bugger looked like he had just survived Juno Beach as he staggered through the door."

Roger added, "But he was OK after a few minutes. I was able to get him laughing—I told him the story about that tea-pail twit from Toronto, who tried to save Algonquin Park from burning up."

Roger was raised in Whitney in a large house on the western edge of town. His parents ran the community post office and rural delivery service for a while, and they occasionally took in boarders for short periods. Roger tells of one guest in their home, a very elderly Algonquin woman, who apparently had no children or immediate family.

She arrived with a strange tale, barely on the edge of believability, and a little cloth bag of gold nuggets, which she never let out of her sight. In the beginning, she was reluctant to talk about her life, but as she came to know and trust Roger's mother and father, she shared some of her story with them.

She described how she had grown up on a dirt farm carved out of the bush near the southeastern Algonquin Park boundary, not far from the Bonnechere River. She was the youngest of a large family of eight or ten kids. She was very close to her father, whose name was Mosie, presumably a variation of Moses. He was a skilled trapper, farmer, and hunter. The family lived a modest life, but was comfortable, with always lots to eat. Their main contact with the outside world was the village of Killaloe. It was there they sold their furs and purchased supplies.

The old lady then went on to tell a story that her father had confided to her a few months before his death.

"One day in November, Mosie was out in the bush checking his traps. He sat down on a windfallen tree beside a little creek to have a rest and a smoke. When it was time to resume his travel, he bent down to pick up his packsack. He was shocked to find a small outcrop of gold under the leaves and woody debris.

"He chiselled off a small piece with his axe. When he went to Killaloe on his next supply run, he was able to determine that it was gold. He exchanged it for supplies. For years after that, he used the gold sparingly and only when absolutely necessary. He apparently had not told anybody except his wife about the location of his discovery, although some of the Killaloe locals were beginning to show some interest."

Before his death, he took his daughter to the site. She described it as being on the edge of a small creek running into the Bonnechere. The head of a rusty old axe was hidden nearby under a stone. As Mosie showed his young daughter the gold vein, he swore her to secrecy. "You are the only one to know about this spot. Besides your own children, you must never tell anybody where it is—especially a white man. It will make him crazy."

Roger explains that the secret apparently died with the old lady. However, at one time there was some unsuccessful geological exploration activity in the area where a large fault starting in the Ottawa area runs northwesterly through the Bonnechere River area.

Roger once had a harrowing Algonquin Park experience—a testimony to his woodsman grit. While working and travelling through a remote area of Algonquin Park in the Redpole Lake area, Roger suffered a major heart attack. His companion, Doug Elliot, was able to call for help on their mobile radio. The AFA's emergency response plan was used by Ontario Air Ambulance Services to locate and pick up Roger with a helicopter. He was transferred directly to a Pembroke hospital and then to the Heart Institute in Ottawa, where he was treated successfully.

Gordon Stewart worked for us for several years in the Achray and Lake Travers areas. He was the first contractor to sign a logging contract with the AFA in 1976. A quiet man with a wonderful sense of humour, he usually drove around on his logging operations in a fully loaded Marquis station wagon. He was also an accomplished storyteller, his speciality being tales of bears invading logging camps.

Bears seemed to follow Gordon around. Sadly, it was his camp at the intersection of the Lake Travers and Crooked Chute Roads that was used as a base camp by military personnel from Camp Petawawa and the OPP in the late 1970s as they searched for three young fishermen. The young men had been tragically killed by a bear at nearby Lone Creek.

Gordon told me of an experience that he had with a bear in one of his logging camps years ago. The loggers would go home on the weekends, leaving the camp unattended during that time. On Sunday afternoons, Gordon would arrive at the camp with a load of supplies and groceries in preparation for the upcoming week. One Sunday he was late and didn't arrive at the camp until after dark. He backed his truck up to the cookery door and with a lighted lantern opened the front door. He stepped inside to come face to face with a huge bear standing upright, his massive snout covered with flour and his jowls dripping with jam.

"The bear had broken through the back door," Gordon explained, "and when I shouted at him, he took off with a snort through the same door with me right behind him swinging a broom. I chased the old bastard through a nearby swamp right into the next township."

I had supper at Gordon's camp one night. Afterwards, I was chatting with him and his wife Margaret in the living room of a house trailer they stayed in at the camp. Margaret stepped into a back room for a few minutes and, as she returned, looked out a window. She suddenly exclaimed, "Gordon, come here and see the cute little bear up the big pine tree." I walked over to the window to have a look as Gordon disappeared quickly into the rear of the trailer.

Suddenly, a loud "bang" resonated from a bedroom window. The bear tumbled out of the tree and scampered unhurt into the bush. There was no such a thing as a cute little bear to Gordon Stewart. At first, Margaret wasn't impressed, but seemed to be satisfied with his explanation that he only intended to frighten the bear, not kill him. "He won't be back," he added.

Firearms are prohibited in Algonquin Park, and only the ghosts at the Achray Work Centre will be able to tell us the real story about Gordon possessing a gun. My guess is that a kindly conservation officer granted him special authorization to keep it tucked under his bed for purposes of protecting his men and cookery. It certainly would not be a practice endorsed by modern-day park authorities.

As a young man, Gordon worked in the logging and sawmilling business with his father, Jake Stewart, a well-known Ottawa Valley personality and raconteur. For many years, Jake was featured on weekend CBC radio programs telling stories about the old days in the logging shanties.

I can recall hearing him one morning marvelling at his city-dwelling radio host, who was so choked with laughter that he could barely continue with his show. "You mean to say," Jake said to him in astonishment, "that you don't know what a dry arse is? Everybody where I come from knows that a dry arse is a potato sack filled with straw. It is used by teamsters to sit on to keep their arses dry while driving their horse-drawn sleigh loads of logs in the winter."

Don Shaw of Shaw Lumber tells a great story about Jake Stewart. Don had picked Jake up at home one day. They were driving into his logging operation to see some of Jake's pine logs, which Don was thinking of buying from him. They met a half-ton truck coming out of the bush and the driver flagged them down. Jake recognized him as a Polish cutter from Wilno he had hired that week.

As Jake rolled down the window, the fellow said to him, "I broke my chainsaw and I need twenty dollars to buy some parts. Can you give me some money to go into town to get them?"

"I don't have any money on me; I'm in the logging business, you know. I haven't seen a dollar in a month," Jake replied. "You will have to go up to my house, and my wife will give you an advance on your wages."

"I have already been there," the logger said. "Your wife said that she won't give me any money unless I have a note from you."

"OK, we'll get you a note," Jake said, as he motioned to Don to get a piece of paper from the dash of the truck and write the note. Don started writing, "Please give twenty dollars to . . . ? What's his name, Jake?"

"I don't know, what's your name?" Jake asked the fellow who was standing beside the passenger window. The fellow gave his name, and Jake repeated it to Don who thought it sounded like Kubesheskie, or something like that.

"How do I spell that, Jake?" Don asked.

Jake turned to the guy and asked, "How do you spell your name?" And then the fun began. "Is it 'es' or 'is'? Is it 'ki' or 'kie'? Hell, he has more skis than Mont Tremblant!" Back and forth the relay went and still no note.

Finally in frustration, Jake shouted to Don, "Never mind his frigging name, we'll be here all day. Just draw his goddamned picture."

"The Odenback Logging Camp is located in Algonquin Park, two haemorrhoids west of the arsehole of Canada."
—*Richard (Dick) Shalla, Odenback Depot logging superintendent, Algonquin Park*

When I first arrived to work in Algonquin Park at Rock Lake in 1962, there were fifteen to twenty, or possibly more, active logging camps situated within the park. This was a carry-over from the J.R. Booth era, when men went to work in logging camps for extended periods and only occasionally came home at times such as Christmas and spring breakup.

However, lumbermen and logging contractors in the 1960s and '70s still wanted their labour force and base of operations to be as close as possible to the logging sites. It was summed up best by the statement made by J.S.L. McRae: "I'm not in the business of trucking men to work—I'm in the business of trucking logs to my sawmill."

Interestingly, when I retired in 2000, there was only one of these camps still operating. It was the Canada Veneers Ltd. Camp (aka Hogan Lake Timber Ltd.), located at Odenback Depot on the old CNR line at Hogan Lake. In latter years, it only operated sporadically in the winter months. I understand that since 2000, the camp has ceased to exist completely and the site has been rehabilitated.

It was at a remote location about a two-hour drive from Pembroke. It had been consistently by-passed for a one-star rating right from the day it received its first layer of tarpaper. The cookery and sleep camp were in the same building and the basement, which frequently flooded during heavy rains, was known as the "Swamp." The rookie loggers slept there. Seniority meant the privilege of a first-floor, one-room suite overlooking the garage and woodpile. The cook's teeth chattered right out of the glass of water and onto the floor when midnight freight trains roared through the depot yard.

Loggers who have stayed at Odenback over the years, and there were many because of the huge turnover, can be placed into two categories. One boasts, "Yes, sir, I am proud to say that I survived a whole winter at Odenback and am a better man for it." The other growls, "I don't want to talk about that godforsaken place. Staying at Odenback would make a stint in Alcatraz feel like a teddy bear's picnic."

This trend in the reduced number of camps occurred in spite of an increased production of forest products from the park between the 1960s and the year 2000. Increased productivity came primarily from the development of modern logging methods and equipment. Consequently, employment levels didn't vary significantly over that period.

There were other reasons for the change. Loggers are like anybody else! They like to play with their babies and weed the backyard gardens in the evenings. The result was that more and more loggers began to commute daily to their jobs, sometimes up to two hours one way.

An upgraded and more extensive road system, the advent of crew cabs, and the improved comfort and reliability of the modern pickup truck all contributed to the trend towards commuting. Meanwhile, logging contractors began to feel the bite of the enormous costs of constructing and operating a camp. There was also the factor of increasingly higher standards of statutory regulations regarding the preparation of food, personal hygiene, and sewage disposal systems. Add to that, where would one find a good bush camp cook in today's world? Tommy Cannon and his mouth-watering cinnamon rolls were a thing of the past!

I have great memories of my nights spent in logging camps over the years. On one notable occasion, the experience was a reflection of the long hours that loggers work and how a logging camp was really only a place for them to sleep, eat, and dry their socks—nothing more!

Ray Townsend and I stayed one very dark winter night at Walter Dombroski's camp at Stewart's Spur. Along with propane support, the camp was powered by a diesel generator that rumbled away at one end of the yard. It was usually shut down at night. Ray and I were bunking in a trailer where the truck drivers slept, next to the bunkhouse. Adjacent to us was another trailer containing a small TV, which laboured to produce one snowy channel. Two small tables were available for the men to play cards on in the evening.

As the generator beside the trailer pounded out its chorus into the dark cold winter night, Ray and I were watching the last few minutes of *Front Page Challenge*. It was shortly before nine o'clock. There was nobody else in the trailer, and just before Pierre Berton identified the last mystery guest, we were suddenly shocked and stunned into an overwhelming horror of silence and darkness.

The end of the world? No, Walter had pulled the switch on the generator for the night. Time for bed was the message!

It was so dark we couldn't even see a wall in front of us. We eventually found the door and made our way across the yard to the truckers' trailer. The next challenge was to find our bunks. With the help of light from some paper penny matches, we stumbled down the hall. But, we couldn't remember an important detail. Were our bunks in the third room from the door or the fourth?

We guessed that it was the third room. The retreat was quick, however, when in the black darkness, I groped along a bunk to find myself caressing a massive truck driver in a deep slumber and snoring like a buffalo.

It made for a great story the next morning at the breakfast table. Walter, laughing at us, commented, "If you guys want to watch TV at night, you had better stay at home with Momma."

In his book *Algonquin Forestry Authority—A 20 Year History*, Ray shared his diary entries describing the sequence of activities in the camp the following morning:

> 4:34 a.m.: trucks start, drivers getting breakfast or their lunch
> 4:54 a.m.: lights come on
> 4:48 a.m.: tractor trailer leaves yard.
> 5:00 a.m.: made my lunch at cookery
> 5:25 a.m.: first bell
> 6:00 a.m.: breakfast

"Everything is funny as long as it is happening to somebody else."
—Will Rogers, humourist

To fail to take a shot at a colleague when the opportunity arises is to miss scoring into an empty net during the seventh game of a Stanley Cup final game. And so with a satisfying grin on my face in the solitude of my office, I am compelled to seize the moment. While the two deserving subjects will agree that these stories about them are basically true, they both grimace when hearing my version of the details. They vigorously maintain that I go beyond reasonable doubt to absolute doubt. The reader can be the judge!

Bill Brown succeeded Joe Bird as general manager of the AFA in 1985. Bill and I had a great working relationship and friendship for twenty-five years. At Bill's retirement party in 1999, I enjoyed describing an experience that we had shared many years before. This is a verbatim account, which I delivered amidst the hail of flying cups and saucers coming from the head table.

Things were not always well in Algonquin Park, and there were some control problems in the early days. A case in point was the time a logging crew got away on the contractor they were working for. They crossed a hundred-foot cleared boundary line adorned with "keep out" signs in twenty-nine languages. Unbelievably, they cut down a few trees on the Petawawa Military Base property.

When I found out about it, I contacted the military immediately. I was told in very clear terms by a "Major Hardtack" to be in his office, the next day at high noon. "Bring your general manager and the chairman of the board of directors," he snapped.

I called Bill and asked him if he had booked his vacation yet, and when he replied, no, I added, "You had better pack a bag, because I think we are going to be doing some time in the hoosegow at Petawawa."

"Not to worry," Bill said. "We will give the major the charm treatment and tell him how important the Canadian army is to national security. We'll treat him to lunch. Before you know it, he will be asking us about the good fishing lakes in the park."

The next day, Bill and I were met by two sentries at the gate and were escorted into Major Hardtack's office. There he was, standing as straight as a poker, six feet five inches of mean and lean, and puffing on a Winston Churchill cigar. I spotted a couple of handcuffs on his desk. A ratty-looking pit bull was lying in the corner chewing on a chair leg.

Standing at the memorial to Joe Bird at the Algonquin Park Logging Museum. Left to right: Brent Connelly, Bill Brown, and Carl Corbett.

Bill started into his charm routine, and by the time he was finished, the security of the planet was dependant on the Canadian army—just about made me sick! Then it was the major's turn. We sat through a three-hour discourse on the theory and practice of control, discipline, and punishment, until finally Major Hardtack announced that the penalty was to be a fine of ten times the value of the "stumpage" of the missing timber.

For those who are not familiar with the term stumpage, it is the value a forest property owner places on standing timber. In those days, Crown stumpage rates were relatively nominal. Bill knew we would be able to handle a fine of that magnitude out of petty cash.

Brent A. Connelly

By this time, Bill had already started his own private celebration. He was tapping his feet with pleasure and winking at me out of both eyes. At that point, the major noticed the jubilation and interjected, "You can hold off on the cartwheels, Mr. Brown. Perhaps I should clarify. That will be ten times my stumpage rates, not yours!"

It was at that point I realized Bill had used up that day's ration of charm. The meeting took a turbulent turn—two sentries escorted us into the meeting, twenty-two escorted us out.

The last thing that I recall about that day was Bill out in the parade square kicking a leopard tank and yelling, "What the hell does Canada need an army for anyway?"

After telling the story, I presented Bill with a plaque adorned with a pair of handcuffs and an inscription from Major Hardtack wishing him the best in his retirement.

As a footnote, I added that Heather had come with me when I purchased the handcuffs at the army surplus store in Pembroke. We were both amused as we left with our purchase to overhear a young clerk say to another, "That old bugger is up to no good."

Bennie Hokum is a highly respected and successful lumberman from Killaloe, Ontario, where he owns and operates a modern, high-production sawmill specializing in smaller-sized logs. It is at the same site as an older, more conventional sawmill. He is well known in the industry for his innovation and initiative in exploring the use of new equipment and methods of sawmilling and logging.

Bennie once hired a logging contractor, the Fellaber Brothers from Lake Clear, who were the first contractors in the area to be equipped with what was at that time a new and revolutionary piece of logging equipment. The feller-buncher was a mobile machine mounted on tracks, equipped with a hydraulic boom and cutting head. It was capable of felling a tree and positioning it for convenient pick up by a skidder.

The contractor was working on Hokum's licenced area off the Achray Road outside the park boundary, and I had visited the job once to observe the machine at work. Eventually, the word got out about the feller-buncher. Many local people working in the forest industry visited the job for a first-hand look.

Carl Corbett, who at the time of writing is the AFA general manager, was at that time our chief forester, based at AFA's Huntsville office. Carl and I worked together for twenty-five years, and once on a timber cruising project in 1975, we narrowly escaped a near-miss disaster during a severe storm while crossing Manitou Lake in a canoe.

Carl called me up one day and asked if I could join him on a trip into Hokum's job. He had some concern that the machine may have the potential to cause damage to residual trees and wanted to see it

Brent A. Connelly

Holy Old Whistlin'

102

for himself. Bob Pick also expressed an interest in seeing the machine, so he came along with us. Carl drove over from Huntsville one morning, and Bob and I met him en route and jumped in with him. To allow Carl to drive his own truck was a mistake. We travelled west up the Achray Road towards the park and turned right onto a branch road into the Fellaber operation. After spending a couple of hours observing the machine, it was time to return to Pembroke for an afternoon meeting. As Carl drove us out to the Achray Road, he was editorializing about the difficulty he was having incorporating the pine marten management guidelines into the forest management plan that he was working on.

With his arms flying wildly inside the cab, as was his custom when telling a story or describing a dramatic event, he was obviously preoccupied and not paying attention to his driving. When we approached the intersection of the Achray Road, I noticed the turn signal was flashing for a right turn, when it should have been left to return to Pembroke.

Hard to imagine! Here was a forester highly trained in orientation skills, and we were heading back into the park. Instantly, Bob noticed the mistake as well and was about to say something when I gave him a poke in his ribs with my elbow. I winked, "Let us see how far we can get with this."

Carl made the turn towards the park as his rant continued, with arms still flying. We drove for a few minutes, and while rounding a turn in the road met a tractor-trailer fully loaded with logs coming out of the park. Of course, to Carl, the truck was on its way back into the park and, of all things, loaded with logs.

"Holy shit," he yelled. "I always thought you buggers from the Ottawa Valley were different. Now I'm convinced. I can't believe you are hauling logs back into the bush. Don't you know that the sawmills are in Pembroke?"

"Not to worry, Carl," I said. "Our contractor, the Jessup Brothers, hired a new truck driver yesterday. And they have him out practising."

"Okay, that explains it, now I feel better," Carl replied with relief, as he turned the truck around and headed back to Pembroke.

"Je pense que le pump est fucké."
—A French-speaking logger employed by Hec Clouthier & Sons Logging Ltd., while attempting to repair his skidder.

Hec Clouthier Sr. was another prominent logging operator who left a huge mark on the forest industry throughout the Ottawa Valley and beyond. Like many others of his era, he began working in the bush with his father at the age of twelve and went on his own at fourteen. He purchased a horse from his father and went to the bush to begin what was to become a very successful business career. He passed away in 2003 at the age of eighty-seven.

He was a short man, quiet most times, feisty at others, and always ready to help the downtrodden, flash a quick smile, and share a logging or hunting story. At one time he owned and operated two logging camps in the Sturgeon Falls area, employing as many as 300 men. For many years, Hec operated logging camps outside Algonquin Park between Deep River and Mattawa, a business his sons continue operating.

He had the nerve of a canal horse and the willingness to try a variety of business ventures, and he did so without apparent fear of failure. The enterprises went beyond logging to include operating a Petawawa dance hall; building, owning and operating a hotel; and breeding and racing a substantial stable of standardbred racehorses. It was during his horseracing days that he and my father-in-law Delbert MacTavish met and became good friends.

In addition to an active business life, Hec presided over a family of ten children, nine of whom were still at home when his wife Molly passed away. Hec's large family is but one example of the enormous size of the broader Clouthier family in the Pembroke and Petawawa areas. Someone once said, "There are as many Clouthiers in Pembroke and Petawawa as there are mosquitos in Algonquin Park on the long weekend in May." For several years, the Clouthier family fielded a baseball team made up entirely of family members and competed in tournaments throughout the Ottawa Valley. Hec was a standout second baseman on that team.

I first met Hec in 1970 in Mattawa when I hired his trucks to haul logs for Weyerhaeuser. We did business together off and on after that, although he only worked for the AFA as a major logging contractor for one year in Algonquin Park. Over the years, my friendship with Hec developed and went on to include his son Tommy, who took over the management of Hec Clouthier & Sons Logging in later years.

One day shortly after our return from the vacation trip to P.E.I. that was made so enjoyable with the company of the Duncan MacGregor audio tapes, Tommy and I were driving together in the bush. We talked about his aging father and how unfortunate it was that the family had no written record of the many interesting facets of his life. I mentioned the tapes that had been made of Dunc. Tommy asked if I would be available to sit down with Hec to try and record some of his life story. Although I had no experience with that sort of thing, I agreed. I had recently retired and was naive enough to think that I would have difficulty filling up my days with useful activity. So much for that absurd notion!

Tommy purchased a good tape recorder, and it was arranged I would go to Hec's home on Tuesday mornings to interview him. On the Monday evening before the first session, Tommy called to advise that his dad was not feeling well, and we rescheduled for the following Tuesday. Tommy told me later that Hec was so intimidated with the thoughts of talking into a recorder that he initially balked.

Tommy persisted and the next week we were underway. Hec lived in a huge old farmhouse on the shore of the Ottawa River between Pembroke and Petawawa. When I knocked on the door, his daughter Leanne, who was caring for him at the time, ushered me into the front living room.

Hec was waiting for me, stiff as a board, sitting on a chesterfield. He looked as if some kind of cross-examination was to unfold. His faithful old spaniel, Freckles, was lying by his feet and a tape recorder sat on a coffee table in front of him. We started by talking about his childhood. It didn't go too well for the first few minutes, while we both tried to brush off the novelty and awkwardness of this new experience.

After about an hour, the old dog, who had been sleeping peacefully at Hec's feet, suddenly jumped up. He began barking and running wildly around the living room in circles. I turned off the recorder expecting that someone had driven into the yard and would be coming in to visit Hec. "No, no," Hec laughed, as he reached behind the sofa to pick up a can of chocolate Rosebuds. "It's treat time for old Freckles. He expects one every morning about this time." After swallowing a mouthful of candy, the old hound laid down once again for another snooze.

Hec Clouthier and Freckles: "No logging today. Gone fishin'!"

That was my opportunity to ask Hec a few questions about some of the dogs he had owned over the years. "Yes, sir, I had some dandies," he boasted, "but Freckles is by far the head of the pack. When the boys were playing baseball, I would send him to where the cooler was hidden under the stands. He would lift off the lid with his nose and bring the players each a beer. Took him nine trips though—he could only manage one beer at a time."

Then, at about eleven o'clock, it was time for Hec and me to have our own treat. He shuffled over to a cupboard in the kitchen and came back with a bottle of Black & White scotch. "Time for a toddy," he said, as he half-filled a couple of water glasses. I would always get my best production out of Hec from "toddy time" until noon, when Leanne would give us another treat consisting of shanty soup, thick meat sandwiches made with homemade bread and, for dessert, hot lemon or apple pie.

After a while we both caught on to the routine. Usually, it was as if we were having a normal conversation and we didn't think about the recorder. However, there were times when there was complete silence. I would check my notes to come up with a meaningful question to ask him during this dead space, oftentimes without too much success.

I recalled Hec telling me a few years before that some of his forefathers may have done some poaching in Algonquin Park. At one point during a lull in our conversation, I remarked that there was a Clouthier Lake in an eastern area of Algonquin Park, and asked if there was any connection between the lake and the poaching activity that he had mentioned. He didn't answer, but stiffened right up with his teeth clenched.

While reaching down to turn off the tape recorder, and with a slipper-covered foot gently rubbing the sleeping dog's back, he looked up at me and asked softly, "Do you want some more ice in your toddy?" I had crossed the line. There was to be no further discussion on that subject.

After five or six morning sessions we finally completed the task, one that I had enjoyed enormously. In spite of my inexperience and the knowledge that we probably missed some important parts of Hec's life, it is satisfying to know that the Clouthier family has some bits and pieces of it as described in Hec's own words.

As Tommy and I chatted for a few minutes at Hec's gravesite outside Pembroke one cold February afternoon, the sadness was softened a little when we chuckled over the thought of Hec pulling out the can of Rosebuds to treat old Freckles, who surely misses him very much.

As I reflect on that time with Hec, I urge anyone with aging parents, grandparents, or just old friends to pick up a tape recorder. Make time to sit down over a cup of tea or even a toddy and start talking. If it doesn't go too well at first, simply ask the question, "Tell me about your favourite old hound." You will be glad that you did and be amazed at the satisfaction and enjoyment that everyone involved will feel.

"Don't criticize logging in Algonquin Park from the comfort of a La-Z-Boy chair in the den of your luxury Oakville home. Lace up your bush boots and come with me to have a look for yourself. I'll show you the real story."
—Barry's Bay logger commenting on anti-logging rhetoric

I don't hesitate for a minute to express my pride in the magnificent work that the Algonquin Forestry Authority has done in the forests of Algonquin over the last quarter of the twentieth century. From its inception in 1975, the board of directors, management, and staff of the Authority, as well as industry clients, have consistently maintained a "come see for yourself" policy regarding forest management activities in the park. Changes in forests over time are tangible, measurable, and assessable against a number of reference points, and it is only by visiting the sites of current and past logging operations that an appreciation of those changes can be realized.

Over the years, off-site public information sessions and various staff presentations and field tours have all contributed to a high level of public awareness. This has generally led to a broad public acceptance of the multiple-use concept for the park. Many road and aerial tours have been conducted, either by special request or by invitation.

Most employees and, on occasion, some directors, in spite of demanding schedules, have contributed their time and expertise in this endeavour. The responsibility does not fall specifically to a few individuals, but rather is shared amongst all. The tours also frequently involve Ministry of Natural Resources and Ontario Parks specialists. The activity is well planned and often customized to satisfy the visitor's interests. The costs of these tours forms part of the AFA's annual public relations budget approved by the Authority's board of directors.

Educators, students, politicians, researchers, environmentalists, scientists, government, and forest industry leaders are but a few who have received tours of forest-management sites. I have been involved in many of these, but there is one that I would especially like to tell you about.

It was a "clandestine" tour for a high-ranking group of German officials in the early 1990s, which had a few senior bureaucrats on Parliament Hill in Ottawa in a dither for a couple of days. Its conclusion remains as much a mystery to me today as then.

During that period, some international concern developed around the perception that widespread clear-cutting practices in Canada were destroying our nation's forests. Some media reports showed some rather dramatic and unfavourable footage depicting a barren forest landscape following logging activity. Environmentalists were kicking up a fuss, and some countries were threatening to boycott Canadian forest products. One of those countries was Germany.

One late Friday afternoon, I was working in my office in Pembroke and received a telephone call from a forester at the federal government's Petawawa Forest Research Station. He explained that a small group of high-ranking German officials was touring Canada and that he had been asked to arrange a tour of forestry operations in Algonquin Park for them. Their arrival was expected within the week, and a full day was allocated for a tour of Algonquin Park.

My initial reaction was to think of the "purple-breasted" bird incident. But clear-cutting was a real and present issue, so after collecting my thoughts, I agreed to conduct the tour under the condition that an aircraft be hired so that the group could fly over the park before going on a ground tour.

Our forest prescriptions and harvesting practices were based on the selection and uniform shelterwood management systems, which involved only the partial removal of trees. Clear-cutting in the park would, therefore, not be an issue. However, I did not want to be accused of taking the

Germans to only select areas and hiding possible embarrassing locations. It was crucial that they have an aerial view to begin with.

It was agreed, and a plane was hired from Pem-Air, an airline based at the Pembroke airport. Then, on the following Friday, I picked up some Heineken beer, as well as German sausage and ripe cheese at Ulrich's, a well-known German deli in Pembroke. I was now ready to meet them early Saturday morning at the Best Western hotel. The group consisted of four German government officials and politicians along with an interpreter and an escort who appeared to be an employee of the Canadian government.

They were travelling in an unmarked van, which at the time did not seem unusual. It may have been a rental. My plan was to fly all morning and return to the Pembroke airport to pick up the vehicles for an afternoon road tour. I asked Heather to join us in the afternoon to give me a hand. Thankfully she did. Not only did she enjoy the day, but she was great company for the two women in the group.

Initially, I had difficulty planning the flight path into the park. There had been previous clear-cutting in areas outside Algonquin, resulting from legitimate prescriptions to manage low-quality poplar stands. I recognized that it would be futile to fly over those areas and try to explain the objectives behind the clear-cutting, especially over an intercom system, which would be competing against the background roar of two engines.

Instead, I instructed the pilots to access the park by flying up over the northwestern boundary of CFB Petawawa (Major Hardtack country). It would have been preferable to fly directly over the base, but the pilots were not permitted to do so because of military regulations.

As we approached the clear-cut areas, which were visible from the left-hand side of the aircraft, I suggested to the passengers that they look out the right-hand side to observe the artillery and tank exercises below. I had prepared some background information on the operations of the base, but before the military documentary was finished, we were in the park. It was time to relax and enjoy the flight. While some might call my navigation strategy that day deceitful, I like to think of it as "Standing On Guard For Thee"!

It was a beautiful, clear summer morning with maximum visibility. We flew for more than two hours and covered the full length and breadth of the park. The aerial view was spectacular, featuring a green carpet of forest for as far as the eye could see. Lakes glistening and sparkling in the sun were occasionally graced with the gentle wake of a slow-moving canoe, while kids could be seen frolicking on the beach at Cedar Lake. We flew over Hailstorm Creek and were treated to the magnificent sight of several moose feeding in the huge marsh. My guests, shaking their heads in amazement, were clearly impressed.

The afternoon ground tour, which followed our delicious picnic lunch on the sandy beach at Grand Lake, was equally successful. I had a small and captive audience who were clearly interested in the science behind the forestry practices used. They peppered me with questions, but as I was so busy managing the tour there was little opportunity to ask them questions in return. About the only thing that I could find out from the escort was that they were at the end of a cross-Canada tour of forestry operations. They would drive that night to Maniwaki, Quebec, and fly home from Mirabel Airport Monday morning.

The tour ended at about four o'clock, and while we were stopped at the park gate to pick up some publications, the interpreter asked if I knew where they could purchase some maple syrup to take home. I remembered seeing syrup for sale at Ulrich's shop in downtown Pembroke and, as it was on their way out of town, I led them there.

It was Saturday afternoon and downtown Pembroke was bustling with pedestrians and vehicles. There were no parking spots in sight, and since they seemed to be in a hurry, I put on the four-way flashers and pulled my truck right up onto the sidewalk in front of the store. I motioned to them to park behind me. I can recall saying to Heather, "If the Pembroke police or parking authority has a problem with this, I'll just have to refer them to the Prime Minister of Canada."

It was like old-home week as the German officials visited with the Ulrich family, and then it was time for us to part company. Our appreciative guests formed a circle around Heather and me on the sidewalk in front of the shop. They thanked us for the tour, and presented Heather with a beautiful scarf and me with a lighter displaying the German national insignia.

It had been a pleasant day for both Heather and me. But as we talked about it that evening, an important question persisted: Why were there no Canadian public figures present to welcome these important people to our region? Conspicuously absent was the Mayor of Pembroke, the local MP and MPP—not even a newspaper reporter or TV cameraman in sight. Very puzzling indeed!

The answer came the following Monday morning. My first call of the day was from the office of the director of the Petawawa Research Station. "Mr. Connelly," the caller said, "I understand that you toured a group of German government officials through Algonquin Park on the weekend." When I replied in the affirmative, a volley of questions followed. Who were they? Where did I take them? What did they see? What questions did they ask and what were their impressions when they left?

After I told the caller that it had been an enlightening day for our guests and that they had left the park apparently favourably impressed, I was asked, "Would you mind explaining what you have told me to a representative of Natural Resources Canada?"

"Of course," was my reply, and within the half hour I received a call from an assistant to the minister in his Ottawa office.

The same questions were asked, but this time they seemed to have a more frantic and urgent tone.

After I assured the caller that our German visitors were happy with what they had observed in the park, he started to quiz me about the escort. "Who was he and where did he come from? What authorization did he have to conduct the tour?"

I told him that all I knew was his name and when I provided it, there was a pause, followed by a mumbled statement to the effect that he was an employee of Natural Resources Canada, but was currently on a leave of absence. "I will have to look into this matter further," he said. I asked him to let me know the outcome of his inquiries, which he promised he would.

That was not to be the first or last unfulfilled promise to be proclaimed from behind the heavy doors of Parliament Hill. The only explanation I can come up with is my own speculation, that the escort was either working on his own in a freelance arrangement with the Germans, or acting on behalf of some other federal government department, perhaps External Affairs.

There have been many interesting wildlife encounters over the years. Charging moose, hungry bear, frightened deer, stranded strippers, purple birds—even a startled partridge who tried to hijack our pickup truck, to mention a few. And then there was a park tour that resulted in a one-on-one adventure with a another turtle, perhaps a cousin to the one that Herbie Hass had worked his magic on.

The wood turtle (*Clemmys insculpta*) is protected under Ontario's *Fish and Wildlife Conservation Act* and is considered to be a species at risk in Canada. In some U.S. states, it is designated endangered or threatened.

A small turtle with a maximum length of 23 cm, it is commonly known as "old redleg" because of the orange or brick-red colour of its legs. It has a distinctive yellow-black underbelly configuration and prefers a wet deciduous or conifer forest habitat. It is found in three ranges in Ontario, one of them being Algonquin Park.

During the last decade, wildlife biologists with the Ministry of Natural Resources and Ontario Parks have actively protected the turtle and conducted surveys to determine its movement and well-being. The program was spearheaded by Norm Quinn, the park's chief biologist. He describes this research in detail in his book *Algonquin Wildlife—Lessons in Survival*. This book is strongly recommended for those interested in learning more about the park's wildlife from an expert. It is extremely informative and also fun to read.

The survey program involved giving captive kits to several people who worked and travelled in remote areas of the park. The kit consisted of a technical sheet providing identification instructions and a blue plastic milk crate. The directions advised that, upon finding a wood turtle, the box was to be placed over the turtle and secured by a stone. Park staff were to be called immediately so that a technician could be dispatched to the site. A hole was then drilled in the turtle's shell and a radio transmitter installed. A three-inch antenna extended from the shell so that the movement of the bionic turtle could be traced.

The AFA was solidly behind the project and, in addition to urging employees to watch for the turtles, also contributed financially to the support of the program. Bob Pick proudly states that he once found one, and others may have been found by other employees and loggers.

I was hosting a tour made up primarily of retired men from the Pembroke and Petawawa area, several of whom had once been loggers. It was a beautiful day in June, the kind of day that turtles are commonly observed laying their eggs on the soft shoulders of the gravel roads. As we were approaching our lunch spot at Lake Travers, I was standing at the front of the school bus explaining the wood turtle program when somebody shouted, "There is a turtle on the side of the road."

What luck. It's show-and-tell time again, I thought, as I motioned to the driver to pull over. I quickly got out of the bus and picked up a nearby stick. I intended to turn the turtle over on its back for proper identification, hoping it was a wood turtle. However, at the very moment I flipped the turtle over, the driver decided to reverse the bus to move it safely onto the side of the road.

Turtle carnage was unavoidable. There was some consolation, however, when the squashed reptile turned out not to be a wood turtle. There also was a slight feeling of relief knowing that I was the only one to witness the blunder, as I had my back to the passengers who were still sitting in the bus. Not surprisingly, I was quick to introduce another subject upon reboarding the bus, after I had announced that the turtle was just a common little snapper. Again not one of my finer moments— probably ranking up there with the Barron Canyon performance!

"Some people waste a lifetime looking for the pot of gold. My needle in the haystack was the search for a long-lost 'donkey steam engine' abandoned in the bowels of Algonquin Park. Then I'll be damned, if I didn't find two of them, all in the same day!"
—E.R. (Ray) Townsend, forester, operations superintendent, AFA

Prior to his employment with the AFA, Ray Townsend had worked a few years for the Wood Mosaic Company of Tweed, Ontario, a hardwood veneer manufacturer. The company had access to timber in Algonquin Park east of Opeongo Lake, and as Ray was responsible for the raw material supply for the mill, he frequently visited the area.

He came to know some of the old-timers in the Whitney and Madawaska areas and was intrigued by their stories of a donkey steam engine, which had been left in the bush between Proulx and Opeongo Lakes in the late 1930s. (A donkey steam engine is a stationary upright steam boiler fired by a small coal-burning firebox and geared to operate a self-contained cable winch. It was used by old-time loggers to pull heavy sleigh loads of pine logs over heights of land.)

Brent A. Connelly

Holy Old
Whistlin'

One winter, a former J.R. Booth camp closed, as it turned out, for good, when the logging season came to an end. At the time it was expected it would reopen the following fall. Anyway, that winter, a donkey engine had been used to winch sleighs over the height of land between the two lakes as the logs made their way overland to Opeongo Lake to eventually be driven down the Opeongo River to the sawmills.

The story was that when the camp did not resume operations the following year, the donkey engine was written off. It was left to rust away into oblivion on top of a hill in a location that only a few old-timers would have known. Upon hearing of this, Ray vowed that someday he was going to find it. That "donkey engine stone" was not about to be left unturned!

In the early days of the AFA, there was not much time for the search. But as Ray approached retirement, he made more time for the project, anxious to get the job done before arthritis came knocking on the door. He began by interviewing René Dubreuil from Whitney, who was in his eighties at the time. He had worked in Booth's camp in 1938 or 1939.

The camp was apparently located near Proulx Lake, and the first thing that Ray set out to do was find the former campsite. He obtained aerial photographs from the National Archives in Ottawa and various Ontario government sources covering different eras. Upon examination he found a clearing, which he assumed to be the location of the former camp.

This was not going to be a "catch-as-catch-can" project. There would be logic applied here. So, in his typical methodical manner, he began to narrow the search systematically. He located the outline and identified the remains of all camp structures on the ground. Then, having been involved in building logging camps before, and with a good general knowledge of the type of camp that Booth had used, he produced a to-scale sketch of the camp layout.

From the sketch, Ray calculated how many men slept in the bunkhouse and, by estimating the width of a horse stall, calculated the probable number of horses in the camp at the time. Then, knowing the approximate distance between the logging area and the point where the logs may have been dumped on the ice on Opeongo Lake, and having calculated the daily log production, he estimated the number of sleigh-load trips per day to the dump. It was then back to the photographs for some site choices along the height of land. His calculations refined the search to two possible locations where old sleigh roads were faintly visible on the old photos.

In 1990, and more than a half century after the engine had been abandoned, Ray set out on the ground search with AFA forest technician Ron Cahill. Ray was twenty-five days away from retirement.

The pair left their truck and began walking through the dense bush. Within an hour, Ray found what he was looking for—and much more. He had arrived at the end of the rainbow and gazed wide-eyed at not one, but two donkey engines. The engines stood like proud twins across the same road from each other. They were in the exact location where they had huffed and puffed the last sleigh-loads of pine logs "up over the big hill." Think about that sight the next time you walk across a white pine floor or sit in an old pine chair.

The winches were in excellent shape, with each having been housed in two separate wooden shacks, which had capsized years before. Beside one winch was a pile of unused soft coal, which had been used instead of wood, the fireboxes being too small to burn wood. The winches were delivered to Whitney, where McRae Lumber Company restored them to their original condition with sandblasting and painting.

Today, one of the winches is housed on display at the park's Logging Museum, while her sister is in protective storage off-site. What a wonderful reminder of an era gone by and a fitting tribute to a man who had the spirit and determination to find them.

Ray Townsend would have made Norman Vincent Peale look like a schoolboy in short pants. It could have been Ray who crafted the phrase "the power of positive thinking," not Peale, and there were plenty of other examples of nothing being impossible for Ray!

One time, we were building some main roads in the Daventry area of the park. Daventry was a former sawmilling community along the CN track several miles "Inbacka Mattawa," not too far up the road from "Inbacka Mackey."

Ray Townsend coming to the rescue of the donkey engines near Proulx Lake, Algonquin Park, 1990.

The road crew was having difficulty finding good gravel deposits, and Ray heard about the problem. He jumped in with his offer of help, promising, "If I can find two donkey steam engines and a prisoner-of-war camp [what a great story this is—more later!] in Algonquin Park, I sure as hell can find you a gravel pit."

Out of the closet came the boots, and a date was arranged. I was staying overnight in Mattawa the night before, and Ray invited me to come along for the day to give him a hand. It was a hot day, and we walked from early morning, up and down hills and through swamps, without any success. It wasn't until three o'clock that we eventually found what appeared to be a beautiful gravel esker or glacial deposit.

Brent A. Connelly

Holy Old Whistlin'

"There it is," Ray boasted, "the mother lode. We are going to celebrate tonight. The steaks are on me!"

(It is important to keep the record straight at this point: When the bulldozer arrived to dig some test holes, that magnificent gravel deposit turned out to be no more than a hill of sand, good for nothing but a beach—probably appropriate for the next part of the story.)

That evening on the trip back to Huntsville, where I was going for a meeting the following day, Ray was good to his word. He led me into South River, where we pulled our trucks up to the front door of an exclusive resort hotel. Immediately, I knew that trouble was looming. We were both wearing bush clothes, much like the day I was told about my welfare cheque, only they were a little grimier and dustier.

We walked into the lobby towards the dining room to find that it was closed. "No problem, Ray," I said. "A quarter-pounder combo at McDonald's in Huntsville will suit me just fine tonight. I'll take a rain check on that steak."

This was not good enough for Ray. He flagged down a waiter racing across the lobby with a tray load of cocktails, who confirmed what we already knew. "The dining room is closed for the day, sir." The waiter paused. "Our guests are dining on the terrace tonight."

"Mmmmm, sounds good to me," Ray replied with a twinkle in his eye, while stroking his chin. "We'll join them."

It was like walking out onto the deck of *The Love Boat*. Elaborately set tables, adorned with colourful linens and fresh wildflower centrepieces, dotted the lawn from the patio down to the sandy beach. Prosperous-looking men wearing ascots and white deck shoes clinked martini glasses with beautiful women, who were flitting about in their printed dresses and miniskirts.

A huge salad bar was set up along one wall, and a couple of chefs visible above the crowd in their tall hats were beginning to fire up the barbeques. And there we were, a couple of Beverly Hillbillies crashing the Academy Awards party. "Hell, Ray," I said, "we can't go out there. They will run us off the gangplank like a couple of stowaways."

"You worry too much, Brent. We'll let on that we are a couple of eccentrics. Besides, I'm as hungry as a bear," Ray replied as we scooted by the maître d' unnoticed. Ray sat down at a table, pulled a folded cloth napkin out of a water glass, and spread it out on his dust-covered knee.

After he had looked around for a minute, he whispered, while giving his chin another stroke, "Mmmmm, looks like it's a help-yourself situation. Let's check out the salad bar, heh, heh, heh." Off we went, with Ray backfilling a plate full of salad like he hadn't eaten since we were at Walter Dombroski's logging camp a few months before.

When we returned to our table we had company. Three startled-looking couples were obviously wondering where in hell did these cowboys come from? After a little small talk, one fellow, thinking that we were probably a couple of misplaced transport drivers off the highway, timidly asked, "Who do you fellows drive for?"

"We drive for the AFA! Heh, heh, heh," Ray replied proudly.

We polished off our huge Alberta T-bones, and then the social part of the evening began. When the effects of the wine began to kick in, our company let their guards down and became wonderfully friendly and gracious. It wasn't too long before the whole table centred around Ray. He was the life of the party. One of the men at our table was a doctor who had practised for awhile in Orangeville, Ontario, which was Ray's hometown. They had many common acquaintances and were enjoying themselves immensely.

But then it was time for me to say goodbye to our new-found friends. As I got up to leave, I said to Ray, "You stay if you like. I have to go to do some work in the hotel tonight in preparation for a meeting tomorrow." At that point, the recreation director arrived at our table with a clipboard. He was scheduling activities for the following day and that evening. The next day featured a tour of a local mine, a float-plane ride, golf, and waterskiing.

The last thing I recall of that evening, as I escaped to my truck leaving Ray with the cheque, was him saying to the young recreation director, "Mmmmm, by Jeez you know, I think I'll sign up for your euchre tournament tonight. It's still early, and the wife is not expecting me home until late, heh, heh, heh." What a man!

"Don't ship me any more logs. I'm full up. There is not enough room in my log yard for two skinny cats to screw."
—Johnnie Shaw, President, Herb Shaw & Sons Ltd.

John (Johnnie) Remick Shaw IV was one of my favourites. He was to the lumber industry as Stradivarius was to the world of violins—a classic creation impossible to replicate. Johnnie, as we all affectionately called him to distinguish him from his nephew John Remick Shaw V, or "Young John," was, in my view, in a class along with people like J.S.L. McRae, Delbert MacTavish, and a few others.

Like many in the lumber and logging business, Johnnie had left school at an early age to help out and eventually take over the operation of Herb Shaw and Sons Ltd. from his ailing father. The company had a timber licence in Algonquin Park and timber limits outside the park, and operated a sawmill and utility pole manufacturing facility between Pembroke and Petawawa. Johnnie was joined

John (Johnnie) Remick Shaw IV at Fraser Depot on the Ottawa River: "Hrmmm, hrmmm. Does anybody want a ride in my airplane to take a look at that nice stand of pine poles? I think I have enough fuel to get us back. If not, we will put down on a good trout lake and fish from the pontoons."

later by his younger brother Donald, and the two formed a well-known tag team in the Ottawa Valley lumber industry for many years, relying regularly on the advice of the youngest of the three boys, Herb, who was a lawyer in Pembroke.

I really don't know where to start to bring Johnnie to life. There was so much to him that a few paragraphs here could serve no more than an introduction. At the very least, I can try to share some of my personal relationship with this remarkable individual. Johnnie was a quiet, shy man, until somebody decided not to live up to a commitment or tried to cheat him. Then the big stick would come out and the fur would fly. In that way he reminded me of Jack McRae, whom he knew and respected.

Johnnie had a tremendous appetite for reading, his favourites being true stories about war, politics, and aviation. And, in spite of a limited formal education, he was intellectually at the head of the pack in many areas. A most colourful man, he could editorialize on a wide range of subjects using homespun vocabulary that was beyond description. If poet William Wordsworth had been able to master an eloquence in profanity, he would have been no match for Johnnie Shaw. It flowed out of him like maple sap out of a cedar spigot on a warm March day.

Johnnie's friendly face was topped by a balding head. His ears frequently served as designated parking spots for a well chewed wad of gum, placed there when he had to give his full attention to delivering a profound statement. This was usually preceded by rising from his chair or the seat of his pickup truck, hiking up his belt, and clearing his throat with a lingering hrmmm . . . hrmmm. This customary warm-up was generally followed by practical and thoughtful words of wisdom or a statement of disgust about some no good, stupid, son-of-a-bitch who "couldn't find two ends of a sawlog."

He was readily recognizable by many in the Ottawa Valley as he humped over the steering wheel of his little green half-ton truck while driving from the sawmill to the mill, and to the bush and back. The dash of his truck was piled high with papers and cigarette packages, cleverly hiding a fuzz-buster, which was always plugged in and ready to sound the alarm.

Johnnie was an accomplished pilot and on weekends could be seen flying his own plane over the log and lumberyards of his competitors to check on their inventories. He could be picked out of a crowd with his ever-present cigarette, high-top workboots, light blue work shirt, and cuffed khaki work pants. The pant cuffs doubled as ash trays whenever he found himself in a no-smoking zone.

He was completely dedicated to the well-being of the Shaw family, their employees, and the operation of the business. Some may have considered him a workaholic, as he commonly worked long hours and weekends. It was in this regard that I was able to score my first points with Johnnie.

In 1975, Joe Bird and I were touring the Pembroke area to meet and introduce ourselves to our new clients to whom we would be delivering logs. It was a task accompanied by varying degrees of tension and apprehension. Here we were, starting up a brand new government agency to take over the logging operations that these people had conducted for themselves under their own direct control for decades. Hrmmm, hrmmm. It's worse than a terror—it's a fright! (—an expression used by Heather's grandfather Rory [Toot] MacTavish when describing a runaway team of horses.)

One of our first stops was to meet Johnnie and Donald Shaw. As we walked into their huge office, where they sat behind adjoining desks, with the walls covered with hunting and fishing trophies, I thought, "Here are a couple of crusty-looking old buggers who are going to put us to the test quickly."

A young Johnny Shaw IV putting his mark on a white pine near Lake Lavieille, Algonquin Park.

Our ace in the hole was Joe Bird, whose outstanding reputation for success in the forest industry had preceded him. However, since it was Johnnie and me who would be working with each other on a day-to-day basis, it wasn't too long into the meeting that I sensed him looking at me. His curious facial expression gave me the impression that he was wondering, "Who the hell is this Connelly fellow from the Soo anyway?"

Holy Old Whistlin'

It didn't take long for the questions to come my way. "Hrmmm, have you had any experience with logging pine sawlogs or utility poles? Where are you from?" He didn't go as far as J.S.L. McRae in asking what my father did, but it was close. When I told him I had worked for Jack McRae his face brightened up a bit.

As we left Shaw's office that day, I asked Johnnie if he could spare a day to come with Bob Pick and me to show us around some of the areas in the park that he was familiar with. He agreed, and a date was set for the following week. We were to meet him at his office at 7 a.m. It was then that I reached back into my bag of tricks and recalled a valuable lesson from Duncan MacGregor: "If you want to impress a lumberman, be sure and beat him to work in the morning, and make it appear that you have been waiting some time for him to arrive."

And that is what Bob and I did. We were in Shaw's yard at 6:30 a.m., and when Johnnie drove in, I had the hood of my truck up checking the tension on the fanbelt. Bob stood beside me watching and munching on his second sandwich of the day. This was not unusual for Bob. His lunch would normally be eaten by ten. By eleven o'clock, he would have his eye on mine.

Johnnie pulled up alongside us and got out of his truck before it had stopped (reminding me of Donald McRae). "Good day for travelling bush," he said without commenting on our early arrival, leaving us to speculate that his thoughts may have been, "Son-of-a-bitch! I must be slipping, being beaten to the job by a couple of government bastards."

That day was the beginning of a wonderful relationship that Bob and I and other AFA people were to have with Johnnie over the years. However, I can recall thinking at the end of that day that, to impress Johnnie Shaw, it was going to take more than beating him out of bed one morning and telling him a few stories about Jack McRae. Personal credibility and the future of the whole venture depended on us delivering logs to him and other client mills on schedule and at reasonable cost. And that is what we did, and I have every reason to believe that the next generation of AFA professionals continues to do so.

There were other times when we were locating new road systems that we asked Johnnie to come along with us to share his knowledge of the region. He was an invaluable resource in helping us chart area that was new to us, but very familiar to him. He seemed to enjoy the opportunity to get away from the scream of the sawmill and undoubtedly saw it as an opportunity to try and influence our choice of logging areas for upcoming operations. "Hrmmm, yes, sir, there is a dandy stand of red pine poles on the other side of that hill. You might want to include that area in your next five-year operating plan. I cut that area back in 1958, and now it is ready for another tickle."

It is with much amusement that I recall one such day with Johnnie, a day that Bob Pick will remember for a long time. We both fondly refer to it as the "pole trailer day." It was the Monday morning after Joe Clark had won the leadership nomination for the Progressive Conservatives at a party convention in Ottawa. I don't recall the year and have no inclination to research the question. I try to avoid thinking about Joe Clark as much as possible these days. Anyway, Johnnie had come with us to help lay out a road near North Branch Lake, an area his own logging operation was developing prior to the AFA's arrival. The preamble to this story was unknown to Bob and me at the time. It wasn't until after the fact that Johnnie would explain how all the pieces eventually fitted together.

In the early '60s, Herb Shaw & Sons owned and operated a small sawmill in Algonquin Park, near Dusk Lake on the road leading into White Partridge Lake. It was the same road we drove that day to access the area we were to explore. The right of occupancy for the former sawmill site was a short-term land-use-permit issued by the Department of Lands and Forests to the company.

One of the terms of the permit stated that when operation of the mill ended, the company was required to remove all structures and equipment, as well as rehabilitate and restore the site to its original state. The company carried out the work as directed, with one exception. The remains of an old derelict trailer used to haul tree-length red pines for manufacture into utility poles had been left behind. It had been pushed off to the side of the sawmill yard and out of sight in the thick undergrowth.

On their final inspection, Department of Lands and Forests staff from Achray found the trailer and served verbal notice to Shaw that he was to remove it from the park. In the meantime, the Shaws had moved all their equipment from the area. Although it was on Johnnie's list of things to do, that particular list was one of many flying around with the pile of papers on the dash of his truck.

A few weeks went by and, after another phone call, still no action. The trailer was becoming a part of the Dusk Lake shoreline. Finally, a written notice arrived at Shaw's office in Pembroke with a stern warning and a deadline for removal. Failure to comply would result in removal of the trailer by the Achray crew, with costs and a monetary penalty to be recoverable from the company.

It was now time to tick this one off the list. Johnnie made arrangements with a small, fly-by-night jobber, who was working for another company a few miles away. "I gave him a hundred dollars," he said, "and told him, 'Haul that son-of-a-bitch of a trailer out of the park and out of my life—it's driving me crazy.'" That would be the last time that Johnnie would hear about that damned old trailer, or so he thought at the time.

Now fast-forward fifteen years to the arrival of the AFA and one of its keenest members, Bob Pick. AFA and MNR had entered into a contractual arrangement to clean up various eyesores in the park, such as old logging camps, abandoned vehicles, and other assorted blemishes on the park's landscape. The program included an inventory of known problem areas, and the AFA engaged its logging or road construction contractors to clean up the sites. The MNR provided the lion's share of the funding for the program. It was a successful undertaking and resulted in some substantial improvements.

One day, Bob Pick was doing an operational inspection of Walter Dombroski's job. He was walking through a remote area about a mile from the former sawmill site, when he stumbled upon an old pole trailer tucked in behind a big rock. "Could it be a twin to the one which Johnnie had hauled away from Dusk Lake fifteen years before?" No, it wasn't a twin; it was the same one, as we were soon to discover. When the puzzle finally took shape, it was apparent that the contractor had not hauled the trailer to Pembroke as directed. Instead, he had pulled it back into the bush with a skidder to be lost forever, supposedly.

In the meantime, Bob dutifully asked Walter to have one of his skidders pull the trailer back out to the main road to a point not far from its original starting position at Dusk Lake. A few weeks later, Johnnie, Bob, and I were on our way to North Branch Lake. I was driving, Bob was in the middle, and Johnnie was pounding the dash of my truck postulating about the future of the Progressive Conservative Party under the leadership of Joe Clark.

We were rounding a corner and suddenly came face to face with the ghost of that old pole trailer. The cat had come back. "Whoa . . . whoa . . . whoa!" Johnnie yelled as he recognized the trailer. "Am I losing my frigging mind? Who was the stupid son-of-a-whore who put that goddamned trailer there?"

"It was me, Johnnie," Bob whispered as he sunk down between the two of us, "but don't shoot me— I just got married last month."

By this time, I had my truck back under control after having, once again, been overcome with laughter. In a few minutes, Johnnie mellowed enough to tell us the whole story, after which he turned to Bob and chuckled, "Don't worry, Bob, I won't shoot you. But you're not going to get one of my sandwiches for your damned lunch."

One of the most challenging and perhaps enjoyable times with Herb Shaw and Sons was each spring when it came time to negotiate sales agreements for the sale of logs to the Johnnie Shaw and Donald Shaw combo. The exercise could easily qualify as a case study in the skills required for effective business negotiations. It was a buffet of hard cold facts relating to national and international financial updates, housing-start statistics, and OPEC strategies, in addition to the occasional yelps of pain, roars of laughter, and a few wild logging and hunting stories.

I would meet with them, sometimes accompanied by Joe Bird or Bill Brown, in their huge office where they sat at their adjoining desks piled high with copies of the *Financial Post*, the *Globe and Mail*, and tons of trade magazines. Not a computer in sight! Just a cup of stubby pencils, which sat on top of large desktop calendar pads. Every once in a while, when a sales rate or a percentage increase popped out of the conversation, a note would be scratched out on a piece of paper and filed under the calendars, to be referred to when needed.

Don, who was mainly responsible for the sawmill operation and lumber sales, was usually attired in a dress shirt, loosely knotted tie, and his trademark designer sunglasses. His role appeared to be to condition or soften up the quest for increases to sales rates. With his feet up on the desk, he would preface the session with reams of facts on workers' compensation and fuel-rate increases, and the deplorable state of the lumber and pole industries. (To make matters worse, Noah wasn't around to build another ark.)

Johnnie, who invariably made the final decision for the company, was the quiet one sitting off to the side, taking it all in. From time to time he would rise out of his chair, hike up his belt, butt his cigarette, park his gum behind an ear, and growl, "Hrmmm, you're goddamned right, Donald. If we have to pay any more than that, we'll have to get out a tin cup and pull up a stool on Main Street in Pembroke."

One particular session stands out for me. It was in the early '80s when interest rates and fuel prices were at record highs. The lumber industry was struggling along with the rest of the world's economy. Shaw's one-storey office, which was located on old Highway 17 between Pembroke and Petawawa, had a main entrance leading to the area where the male-dominated office staff worked, and at the other end of the building was the large office that Johnnie and Don occupied. This office was serviced by a separate entrance, which was often mistaken by newcomers as the entrance to the main office area.

During that period of extreme austerity, Shaw's had entered into a retail arrangement with a Home Hardware store located next door. A customer of the store wishing to buy a few pieces of lumber to tie on to his car roof-top carrier would pay the cashier in the store and receive a voucher. He then went over to Shaw's to pick up the purchase.

I was in the office working out some rates with Johnnie and Don when, in the middle of one of Don's rants, an old fellow walked in the door carrying a piece of paper. Johnnie got out of his chair and ushered him into the outer office to be helped, and as he came back in, he apologized for the interruption. He explained the arrangement with Home Hardware.

A few minutes later, just as Donald was building up another head of steam, a lady came in the door carrying a piece of paper. Once again, the meeting was interrupted as Johnnie took her to the next office. He returned and, suddenly, Don jumped out of his chair. I swear they both said it at the same time, "There you are, Brent. You have seen it with your own eyes. The goddamned lumber business is so bad these days that we are down to selling one board at a time."

Was it staged or rehearsed? Not a chance! Did they seize the moment? Hrmmm, hrmmm, you bet they did!

Earlier, I mentioned the benevolence and compassion that many loggers and lumbermen extended to their employees and to the community at large. I became aware of several real situations involving men like Jack McRae, Walter Dombroski, Ed Wunsch, Hec Clouthier, Gordon Stewart, and many others. These men were hard-working, tough-dealing, rough-talking, and sometimes just plain ornery, but the face of kindness was never very far below the surface of the grit. Johnnie and Donald Shaw ranked high as special men when it came to quietly performing acts of caring and giving of themselves—doing God's work, so to speak.

Residents of the Pembroke and Petawawa area will tell you the Shaws provided summer employment in their lumberyard, office, or mill to many teenagers who were aspiring to go on to university or college. These were generally youngsters who may not have been able to count on much financial support from home. I have been told that, at times, the number of students employed in the summer may have exceeded need.

The thought of this practice reminds me of a story Don once told me about Johnnie. Young John, who was Don's son and Johnnie's nephew, was a mere wisp of a boy until he was about sixteen. Overnight, he sprouted like a dandelion to become a six-foot, two-hundred-pound linebacker. That was the year that John's name changed from Little John to Young John.

One day he was working on a lumber pile in front of the office and Johnnie was at the window watching the men working. He pointed to Young John and asked Don, "Who the hell is that young lad out there on the lumber pile. By Jeez, he looks familiar."

"That's your nephew, Johnnie," Don laughed.

"Well, I'll be damned," Johnnie replied. "You must be feeding him fertilizer."

Orme Dennison passed away a few years ago in his early nineties. He had been raised at Lake Dore not far from where John Shaw II had built a sawmill and grist mill in the mid 1800's. To this day, the Shaw family has maintained a connection to the area and especially to the people descending from the original residents. Orme was a colourful character, having worked at a number of things throughout North America in his lifetime. He was a favourite of Johnnie and Donald.

Heather was involved in visitation outreach activity with elderly people in Pembroke, and I went along with her one day to visit some residents of a local nursing home. It was here that I met Orme. He had been a logger and had sold heavy equipment at one time. We had much in common and quickly found ourselves having an enjoyable conversation. The subject of the Shaw family came up, and old Orme told me the following story, with the trace of a tear forming in the corner of an eye.

For a few years Orme made his living as a mechanic, working on cars and half-ton trucks in a detached garage behind his house near Lake Dore. It was a solid structure set on a concrete slab and was equipped with the latest tools and equipment. I don't recall the details, but one day he was involved in a bad accident and suffered a broken leg. It must have been a serious break, as he was hospitalized for several days.

A day or so after the accident and while still recuperating in a Pembroke hospital, poor Orme's garage burned to the ground. His only livelihood at the time gone up in a billow of smoke. Things looked bleak for Orme and his family. However, within hours of the fire, Donald and Johnnie had gathered up some lumber from their yard inventory, assembled a few men from the mill, and began rebuilding Orme's garage. When Orme came home, there it was in the backyard—a brand-new garage, complete with enough tools to get him back on his feet. I can still see the gratitude shining from Orme's weathered old face as he told me his story that day.

Throughout my twenty-five years of doing business with the Shaw family, I learned of many other similar humanitarian acts. The accounts of these deeds were always by subtle word of mouth and never through splashy reports. For them, it was not a matter of seeking credit. It was simply a matter of helping out the other fellow.

Just up the road from where Orme lived at Lake Dore, the Shaws retained ownership of 600 acres of forest land, which had been owned by the family since 1847. Within that forest were 120 acres of outstanding old-growth hardwood forest, and in the mid 1970s, the family turned the property over to the National Museum of Natural Science and the Nature Conservancy of Canada. This protected area now stands as a legacy to the founding generation of Shaws who arrived in Canada from Scotland in 1826. It will forever remain a preserved area for the purposes of scientific study and outdoor education.

On June 19, 1979, a dedication ceremony was held on-site, which was followed by a reception in a nearby Lake Dore hall. Donald, Herb, younger sister Mernie, their mother Grace, and their families were there that day, along with a number of invited guests and dignitaries. Everybody was there except Johnnie who, because of his shy nature, was not usually given to formal ceremonies or celebrations.

He had other things to do. When asked why he wasn't there that day he replied, "We gave away our best bush, so I had to go looking to buy another one." That was typical of Johnnie Shaw. However, you can bet a load of logs that his chest swelled with pride that day, albeit from a distance.

There was another characteristic that could describe the logging contractors and lumbermen that I have worked with over the years, which I am compelled to share at this opportunity. That is their culture of honesty, integrity and fairness, unfamiliar terms in these days of outrageous government scandals and corporate acccounting fiascos. It is with pride that during more than three decades of establishing contract and sales rates, negotiating these rates and signing contracts, not once was there even a suggestion or an inference relating to bribery or patronage.

Profane words and hard arguments were always present, but at the end of it all, there were handshakes and a contract—and people went to work. Joe Bird and I were talking about this one day when he made a typically simple and profound observation. "Loggers are like farmers," he said. "From the time they rolled out of their cribs as tots, they were taught through the example of their parents that success in business had to be earned. It could only come from working hard and working smart. It could never be purchased, and to hand a cheque to a crocodile would be to risk having an arm chewed off. And when was the last time you have ever heard of a crooked farmer?" He was right—at least I have never met or been told about one.

During the last four years or so of his life, Johnnie was burdened from the effects of a stroke, causing him some paralysis and speech loss, but leaving his mind as sharp as ever. He continued working every day and was frequently seen driving his little green half-ton truck around the mill and pole yard. Don had passed away by then and it was time to hand the reins over to John and Dana of the next generation of Shaws, to whom he continued to provide his wise guidance on major decisions.

One day during the last week before my retirement, I received a call from Dana. "Johnnie would like to see you," he said. "Can you come up to the office?" When I arrived at the office, Johnnie reached into a paper bag and pulled out a beautiful hand carving of a logger working on the log drive with a pike pole in his hands. He had always enjoyed hearing of my experience losing out on the working-man's lunch that first day of the river drive back on the Rouge.

Without a word, but with his eyes saying farewell to me, he handed me the carving. He shook my hand, shuffled out to his truck, and drove away towards the garage. He probably went to check when repairs to a front-end loader would be finished. The next time I saw Johnnie was in the Pembroke General Hospital, where he lay gravely ill a couple of weeks before his death in 2001. Dana told me later that Johnnie had driven by himself to Renfrew to purchase that carving from a local craftsman.

The First Presbyterian Church in Pembroke was full for Johnnie's funeral service, during which a beautiful tribute written by his admiring sister Mernie was read. The words flowed around the Frank Sinatra tune "I Did It My Way." He had many friends and had accomplished much and, yes, he was a free spirit. He did it his way, and for that reason all of us who knew him will remember Johnnie affectionately for a long time.

It was a beautiful sunny day with a chorus of birds singing in the background in that pretty little cemetery on the shore of Lake Dore. As a group of us walked away from Johnnie's gravesite, we exchanged our own personal stories about him. It was an opportunity to tell my favourite one to his niece Lisa, her family, and a couple of friends. It is a story requiring a somewhat fragmented preamble, so please bear with me.

Those of us who knew Johnnie Shaw knew he was not one to come home from a long day at the mill or in the bush to log onto the Internet in search of government Web sites outlining the most recent developments in statutory regulations affecting the lumber industry. His preference would be a good American Civil War book. That other stuff was left to Donald, John, and Dana to sort out.

It was not that Johnnie wasn't prepared to comply with these regulations. It was just that he didn't feel it was necessary for him to be at the front of the line to hear about them in the first place. His intolerance for unnecessary delays in getting the job done and his results-oriented nature frequently caused regulations and permit applications to receive a mere quick glance.

I was told of one such example when Johnnie undertook to install a culvert leading into his mill yard from a Renfrew County road. He didn't need a ten-page permit to tell him how to install it properly. He knew how to do it. The Shaws were well known in the industry as being good operators. Their mills and lumber and log yards were neater than most, with trucks and other rolling stock always clean and in a good state of repair.

While Johnnie was installing the culvert, a county official appeared on the scene. He severely scolded him for doing the work without the necessary permit containing the appropriate regulations and conditions. "You'll have to talk to my legal department in Pembroke about that," Johnnie said. "I don't have time. There is a load of gravel coming to cover the culvert and I need to arrange to have it spread." Of course, his legal department would be none other than kid brother Herb residing in his downtown law office. There may have been other times over the years when Herb was called on to deal with matters of this nature, I'm not sure. You would have to check with him.

It was always amusing when, occasionally, Johnnie would get tangled up in the vernacular, especially when he was excited. He could take words, names, and descriptions from far-right field and put them in at shortstop in a manner that would make your head spin. For example, the CBC's national newsanchor was Lloyd Mansbridge, supposedly making his counterpart on CTV Peter Robertson. "It wouldn't take long for those Petawawa Airborne lads to smoke out that son-of-a-bitch of a Saddam Kdaffy from his root cellar." We always understood what he was telling us, but sometimes the unusual packaging would make it interesting.

I and my colleagues belonged to the Ontario Professional Foresters Association. The OPFA was initially created in 1957 under the *Professional Foresters Association Act* to protect the public interest in providing a regulatory framework for the work of foresters in Ontario. In 2000, provincial legislation established it as the licensing body for professional foresters in the province. For many years, professional foresters have used the letters RPF following their names to provide the designation of Registered Professional Forester. At times, they are casually referred to by others as "those RPFs."

One day Young John was scheduled to attend a meeting with a couple of foresters employed by the Ministry of Natural Resources. The purpose was to resolve an issue between the MNR and Herb Shaw and Sons. As John was leaving the office to go to the meeting, Johnnie cautioned him, "Hrmmm, hrmmm . . . now don't you be taking any bullshit from those RSPs."

In 1983, a violent wind and rainstorm ripped through the eastern regions of Algonquin Park, causing major damage to magnificent stands of white and red pines. Large, mature trees with their root systems still attached were blown down, causing varying degrees of devastation over an area of about 5,000 hectares. In some areas, one hundred per cent of the trees were either levelled or seriously damaged beyond recovery. Within days of the storm, we had deployed all our logging contractors in a massive blowdown salvage operation.

The plan was to salvage as much valuable timber as possible before deterioration set in and to get planting underway. Foresters are accustomed to reminders of nature's authority such as this but, nevertheless, the feeling of loss that we all had was deep and widespread. Johnnie lessened the gloom, however, when we met a couple of weeks after the storm and he asked me, "How are you fellows making out with that 'big blow job' up in the park?"

Most people who have worked in an industrial or commercial workplace will be familiar with a program called WHMIS, which is an acronym for Workplace Hazardous Material Information System. It is a universal system designed to reduce the risk of hazardous products in the workplace and is governed by federal and provincial laws. In Ontario, the responsibility for enforcement rests with officials of the Ministry of Labour. The WHMIS program centres largely around the proper signage of hazardous material and the mandatory training of workers in the safe handling of these materials. It is an excellent program and a very important tool in maintaining a safe workplace.

WHMIS came into effect at a time when sawmills producing pine lumber were still using what was called the "dip tank." To protect pine lumber from staining and discolouration and eventual downgrading, boards coming out of the mill on to the boardway passed through a tank containing a preservative chemical. Workers stationed near the tank were outfitted in rubber gloves and aprons for their protection. (Modern-day sawmills no longer use the in-line dip tank. The process is now done with front-end loaders dipping packages of lumber into stand-alone tanks situated away from the main mill and its employees.)

Anyway, on to the story, one that I consider to be a classic.

Early one morning I was driving into the park when Johnnie's green truck shot by me like a bullet. However, as he passed, he motioned for me to pull over. It was obvious he had something on his mind. He parked up the road and waited for me while I caught up to him. His smoke-filled truck was worse than any Chicago pool hall could be and, as I climbed in beside him, the rant started.

"Brent, you know who is running my business these days?" he asked. "It's a bunch of fuzzy-chinned little bastards working for the government, running around shoving their frigging rule books in my face, telling me what I can or can't do. They don't know a sawmill from a whorehouse, but yet they are telling me that I need authorization for this and approval for that. Twenty-page permits and all kinds of other bullshit. If I don't have everything approved, they will write me up or shut me down.

"Son-of-a-bitch," he growled, "I'm not steering my ship anymore. No, sir, I'm nothing more than a goddamned deckhand peeling potatoes for the cook."

"Is it that bad, Johnnie?" I asked.

"Bad! You better believe it!" he said. "A couple of weeks ago, I got a call from Ronnie Charles at the mill. He told me that some little prick from the 'Board of Works' [aka Ministry of Labour] was going to shut the sawmill down because I didn't have a sign near the dip tank. My lads have been working around that tank for years. They all know the chemical that is in it and how to handle it—I make sure of that. When I got the call, I jumped into my truck and went over to the mill. I told that little bugger, if it's signs you want, I'll put enough signs up that you will be able to read them from Eganville, and I did.

"Hrmmm . . . hrmmm, but that wasn't the end of it," he added. "Yesterday, I had to shut my whole operation down for the morning so that the men could take a training course. I'm not sawing logs anymore, I'm running a goddamned university. It cost me over three thousand dollars. Can you believe that?"

To this point I hadn't said anything. I felt some empathy with him, as I had frequently heard the same complaint about over-regulation in the industry from various sources.

Finally, he paused for breath, and I commented, "That is WHMIS you are talking about, Johnnie."

"Don't know his name," he snapped. "He was a little sawed off son-of-a-whore with a moustache."

Our daughter Kathy is the Occupational Health and Safety Co-ordinator for Canadian Blood Services in Ottawa. I have suggested to her that the next time she conducts a WHMIS course and finds herself with some stiff and unfocused participants, tell that story. That will loosen them up.

What a great reminder that story is, that at the other end of government-created regulations, there are always real people trying to sort it all out and survive. Loggers, lumbermen, and farmers can tell you all about that!

Chapter 7—Time to Whittle a Stick

"The logs have been delivered to the sawmill. It's time to rest, bait a hook, and whittle a stick."

—Brent Connelly, forester

They can be seen in many small communities and rural areas surrounding Algonquin Park: weathered old loggers sitting on the back stoop, spitting in the dust, and whittling a stick. "Old Yeller" lies contently at their feet, happy that the master is with them every day now, not only on weekends. And if a neighbour or friend drops by for a visit, chances are they would be treated to a "loggers' lament."

"I mind the time back in the early fifties when we were cutting big white pine 'Inbacka' Achray. There was some nice young pine trees coming up then. Boy, I sure would like to go back to see how they grew. I'll bet they are towering giants now."

Another version might be: "Yes, sir, back in 1964 I was running a D7 bulldozer for McRae. We were building roads near Whatnot Lakes, and Paul Kuiack had laid out a road to cross a big mountain. Well, sir, I had to move boulders half the size of my dozer to get up that hill. Talk about tough going! I worked for two days to build a distance from here to Gary Cannon's woodshed over there. Someday, I am going to return to see how the trucks are making out hauling 'up over that big hill.'"

And so it goes—loggers wanting to go back and have a look at where they worked decades before. This always intrigued me because I shared the same feeling many times. And so, like Ray Townsend, there was also something I wanted to do before leaving Algonquin Park for the last time. I planned to allocate a few dollars from the public relations budget and treat some of these old guys by loading them onto a bus one day and taking them back in time. As a bonus we would have some fun, too.

I had lived in Pembroke, Whitney, and Mattawa while working in the park and knew many of the oldtimers living there. These communities were to be the focus for the nostalgia tours. In 1997, we toured a group from Pembroke and, in 1999, some old loggers from Whitney. I was planning to do the same for the Mattawa area but, regrettably, didn't have enough time to pull it off before my retirement date.

I had sensed that many retired loggers may have become forgotten men left to sit on the back stoop, their knowledge and experience an untapped resource. And so, from a public relations aspect, these men would make credible spokesmen in their communities regarding the state of the park's forest. They had been there in the beginning and were more qualified than many observers to describe the changes in the forest over the years. They loved the bush and understood it. They had an appreciation for wildlife and the beauty of the lakes and waterways of Algonquin Park. Their assessment of the present condition of the forest should be unquestioned.

It was early on a beautiful September morning in 1997. An assorted group of retired loggers, contractors, forest industry managers, and others who had once worked in Algonquin Park gathered in the log yard at the Shaw sawmill outside of Pembroke. A couple were armed with canes. Many were a little more bent and stooped than the last time I had seen them. But they all had one thing in common. Each face was smiling as they chatted, greeted, and shook hands with each other.

The group of twenty older men waited excitedly like a bunch of school kids. A yellow school bus was to be our time capsule for the day, taking us into the past, while highlighting the present and arousing speculation and hope for the future. We looked back through stories and bus stops to observe various silvicultural treatments and logging operations. There was even a "working-man's lunch" and no shortage of tall tales.

One of the most enjoyable things for me was the enhanced appreciation of park history that I acquired that day. Occasionally, an old fellow would jump up and point out the window of the bus to a small clearing or even some dense bush and exclaim, "I mind there used to be an old jobbers' camp there back in the fifties." Another told us, "We once dumped logs into the Petawawa River at that spot for the log drive down to the Ottawa." I had not been aware of a couple of former sawmill sites that were also pointed out to the group that day.

Walter Dombroski was with us that day. As we drove over the CN railroad right-of-way at Radiant Lake, he pointed down the track to an opening in the bush. He explained that a railway batch-camp had once existed there. Walter reminisced about having worked there as a section hand for the CNR when he was a boy of eighteen, nearly fifty years before. There were no roads then, and the only way to and from the camp was by rail.

"We worked like dogs all day," Walter stated proudly, "and then had to go back to the shack and make our own grub. We ate lots of fresh trout and," he added with a smile, "the odd 'choice' steak that you would not expect to find in the meat department at the IGA in Barry's Bay today."

Walter then went on to tell us about some of the poaching activity that had been done by a few of the older and more seasoned railroad hands during those days. The foreman of the crew at one time was a notorious poacher. He was responsible for a large section of track and travelled up and down the line from one location to another. Walter's crew would only see him occasionally, perhaps once a week, but wherever he went, he had his canoe with him. It was his calling card, and he was seldom seen without it.

The foreman was in cahoots with a couple of the men in Walter's crew. They trapped and shot beaver in their spare time and passed the harvests onto the old foreman. He, in turn, marketed the pelts by sending them out on the train to a trapper in Pembroke, the fourth member of the gang.

One Sunday, the two railway workers were in their boat on Radiant Lake checking their traps. In the distance they saw a motorboat approaching from the north end of the lake.

"Son-of-a-bitch, it's the game warden," one shouted, as he threw a beaver carcass overboard hoping to get rid of the evidence in time. Both knew if they were caught poaching, not only would there be heavy fines involved, they would also lose their jobs. The beaver carcass didn't sink, so they stood up in the boat and tried to push the animal under the boat with their oars. After their first try, they thought that they had succeeded, only to find the animal had resurfaced on the opposite side of the boat. Finally, out came the hunting knives, and the beaver was cut into pieces before sinking below the surface.

In the meantime, the boat was approaching rapidly, so they reached for their fishing rods to make it appear that they were out in the lake for a leisurely and legitimate Sunday afternoon fish. Suddenly, they remembered that their rifle was in the bottom of the boat. With no place to hide the illegal firearm and with the speeding motorboat almost upon them, the last piece of evidence—the rifle—had to be disposed of. In a state of panic, it was thrown into the lake.

As the motorboat slowed down to approach, their hearts sank to the bottom of Radiant Lake along with the rifle. Holy old whistlin'! The lone occupant of the boat was not the game warden after all. It was the leader of the pack himself, the old foreman, who had traded his canoe in for a motorboat.

The foreman pulled his shiny new boat up alongside theirs and smiled, apparently pleased that his crew was on the job. He then asked, "Do you have any pelts for me today, boys? Business has been a little slow lately."

It has been said that, from time to time on a quiet and still Sunday afternoon, their response can still be heard booming off the hills surrounding Radiant Lake.

To this day, the treasured rifle lies peacefully at the bottom of the lake. When we asked Walter if he knew the approximate location where it was thrown overboard, he replied quickly and insistently, "Don't know, wasn't anywhere near the lake that day. I was back at camp reading the Bible all afternoon."

As my thoughts peek back into the history of the CN and to Walter Dombroski and some of the stories told that day, I am reminded of another trip two years later. In 1995, CN discontinued the use of its rail line through Algonquin Park and began removing the track. During this time, it was possible to travel on the right-of-way by truck, even though CN restricted travel for liability reasons.

Bridge trestles remained in good shape for a couple of years, and with the exception of a few minor washouts, it was possible to safely drive from Achray to beyond the northern boundary of the park to the Bonfield area, south of North Bay.

Danny Janke and I planned on travelling the route. We wanted to explore certain sections of the track, with the thought that future temporary logging roads could cross the right-of-way in certain locations. Since there would be no more trains operating, we thought we could make an argument to the park superintendent for that possibility.

A date was set in the fall of 1999. Since Walter Dombroski and Johnnie Shaw both had a long history of working on and using the railroad for shipping logs, we invited them along for the trip. The scenery was outstanding and featured a shoreline view of major waterways, such as the Petawawa River, Radiant Lake, and Cedar Lake.

Walter Dombroski, aged eighteen, at the Acanthus CNR work camp, Cedar Lake, Algonquin Park, 1953.

Walter had brought along a small black-and-white photo of himself that had been taken in 1953 when he was working on the railroad. The eighteen-year-old Walter was leaning against a signpost designating "Acanthus." This was a former section-crew work centre in a remote area on the northern shore of Cedar Lake. As we approached the lake, Walter began looking for the site and with his remarkable memory was able to identify the exact location of the former sign. Only a small pile of stones remained to mark the spot. It gave me great pleasure to take a picture of Walter standing at the same location where he had once stood as a youth nearly five decades before.

On that trip, we became so carried away with the thrill of driving where trains had once roared through the Algonquin landscape that we drove the full length of the park only to become lost for awhile in the Bonfield area. We didn't arrive home that night until close to eleven o'clock. Some might assume we would have been greeted at home that night by rather anxious wives, but they will tell you that, over the years, they have become conditioned to expect that, once in awhile, their men will be overdue when they are having a good time "on the job."

Walter Dombroski, aged sixty-four, at the same site, 1999.

There were many highlights to the Pembroke nostalgia tour, but none more captivating and enthralling than the outcome of a casual conversation between two very spirited and interesting men. Both were retired, well known, and respected in forestry circles in Eastern Ontario and West Quebec. Ray Townsend and John (Bud) Doering had known each other for years, having done business together buying and selling pulpwood and sawlogs. Their relationship was largely of a

Pembroke Nostalgia Tour, Algonquin Park, 1997. From left to right: Yvon Soucie, Dick Shalla, Paul Hildebrandt, Bert McKenney, Brent Connelly, Danny Janke, Bud Doering, Walter Dombroski, Wayne Pearson, Augie Stencell, Al Purdy, Augie Stresman, Gordon Stewart, Alfred Vietinghoff, Don Smith, Bud Wahl, Art McNair, Roger Mask, Bob Pick, and Ray Townsend.

Pembroke Nostalgia Tour, Lake Travers, Algonquin Park, 1997: Tailgate Luncheon. Left to right: Paul Hildebrandt, Jeff Driscoll, Roger Mask, Augie Stresman, Walter Dombroski, and Danny Janke.

business nature, but that was about to change when they found themselves sitting beside each other on the "nostalgia" bus that day.

Bud was raised in the village of Brent on the northern shore of Cedar Lake in Algonquin Park. The village, which has been reduced to an outfitting store and a few summer cottages, was once the year-round residence of several families. The CNR and a former sawmill were the source of employment for the community. Bud left Brent at the age of sixteen to attend school in Pembroke, and went on to become a logger and logging camp foreman with Gillies Bros. Lumber Company and later held senior positions in the Woodlands Division of the Consolidated Bathurst Inc. pulp mill at Portage du Fort, Quebec.

Bud, a quiet man with a gentle sense of humour, has served as reeve of Horton Township, where he makes his retirement home while doing part-time forest management work on his woodlot. Five minutes with Bud Doering is all one needs to be impressed with his knowledge of the bush and the people who work in it.

As the bus bumped its way up the Lake Travers Road, Ray shared with Bud some of the discoveries he had made while writing his book about the history of the Algonquin Forestry Authority. He noted that two World War II prisoner-of-war camps once existed in Algonquin Park, one being Standard Chemical Camp No.10 in Paxton Township, the other the Gillies Bros. Spring Camp on the Nipissing River, which flows into Cedar Lake. Bud knew the Nipissing Spring Camp well. As the conversation continued, they asked me for a map so that they could determine the approximate location of the camp. I could almost see what was unfolding.

They looked at each other and wondered, "Do you suppose we could still find the location of that old camp?" It didn't take long for the suggestion to kick into action. That night, Ray was in our Pembroke office pouring over aerial photographs and plotting the course. It wasn't a donkey engine, but it was close.

Imagine two retired men: Ray in his early seventies and Bud in his late sixties, about to lace on the bush boots once again. They loaded up their packsacks and tramped off into the bush of Algonquin Park in search of an old logging camp that no longer existed and that only one had seen—and that was more than fifty years before!

The following is an account of their trip to the Spring Camp as recalled by Ray Townsend:

> On October 2, 1997, Bud left Renfrew, I left Port Sydney, and we met on Highway 17. Together, we travelled the bush roads to the nearest point possible to the Spring Camp site. The trek through the bush on a compass bearing was arduous, the distance long, the bush dirty, and it was trying to rain. On the way Bud told me the following interesting story.

Bud's father was a long-time Gillies employee. Almost every summer the company was able to offer young students part-time summer employment. Bud was always ready and willing to accept any type of work offered. Gillies had a depot on Cedar Lake at Brent; the Doerings lived at Brent.

This particular year, the summer of 1945, the company had a keep-over man at Spring Camp and another lone dam-keeper at High Falls on the Nipissing. The two men kept in contact with each other and the company depot at Brent on a regular basis using the treeline telephone. Occasionally the men would walk down the tote road for a gabfest.

One day, after several calls to Spring Camp with no response and no answer the following day either, the man at High Falls decided to visit his neighbour. The worst of his fears was realized when he discovered the man dead on the bales of hay in the hay shed. He immediately reported his finding to the depot and requested they send a wagon to pick up the body. A box wouldn't be necessary; he would make one.

Fourteen-year-old Bud Doering and a teamster were soon on their way. Bud well remembers arriving at the windowless log hay shed with its door chained and locked; inside blowflies buzzed around the corpse. This they rolled into the box and soon were on their way.

Luckily my compass bearing was good and we hit the east side of the campsite. Searching through the young trees we eventually stood in front of what must have been the hay shed. There was basically nothing left of the other buildings—just a square outline of their foundations, the dirt heaped up to help keep the air out of the first row or two of logs.

The front of the hay shed, although leaning, was still intact; even the chain on the door was still there. This, as Bud explained, was necessary to keep the settler teamsters who had their own teams in camp from stealing extra oats for their horses. As soon as Bud saw this old door with its rusty chain it brought back a flood of memories.

"Yes, Ray, this is the hay shed. Well I remember."

A tip of the hat to both these fine men! There would be no sitting around blathering over the past, sipping tea, snacking on arrowroot cookies, and playing checkers in a dingy drop-in centre basement for these two. Not a chance! Reliving the past for them meant putting on the old boots and stepping back into it. Some lessons to be learned about life here!

As a footnote, it seemed that Ray Townsend was always searching for something, either a prisoner-of-war camp, a donkey engine, or his next feed of liver and onions. In 1995, he accompanied a group of World War II veterans on a nostalgia trip to Holland, where he found an old railroad station where he had manned a Bren gun position shortly before an attack from German tanks. He was slightly wounded during the skirmish.

The Whitney nostalgia tour began one evening with a visit to Phil Roche. Over a pot of tea, we scanned the telephone book to find out who was still living and who might be interested. Phil and Maxie Shalla made the contacts, and a date was set for early October of 1999. The proposed route of the tour was to be the Lake Louisa area, although not close enough to the lake to check if the rock

Bud Doering beside the remains of a water-tank sleigh at the Spring Camp on the Nipissing River, Algonquin Park, 1997.

was still leaning up against that old yellow birch tree. Forester Bill Hubbert, who was AFA's Huntsville area supervisor and who had extensive knowledge of the forest management treatments applied in the area, offered a day of his time to help. A school bus was hired, and Elva Gorgerat made us a huge working-man's bush lunch. It consisted of thick ham and turkey sandwiches topped off with a slice of cheddar, butter tarts, date squares, and fruit for dessert.

Fifteen men showed up at the bridge in Whitney that morning. Phil had given me a list of who was expected to attend beforehand, and I had worked with, or at least known, most of them. It had been thirty-four years since I had seen them but, surprisingly, I was able to identify them all. They may not have stood as straight as they once did, but they had not changed that much. A lifetime of physical work appeared to have kept them quite fit.

Included in the group was my old boss Donald McRae. It sure was great to see him again after all that time. As some were fairly elderly, we were concerned with how best we could respond to a possible medical emergency. The bus was not equipped with a mobile radio, so John McRae offered to follow us in his radio-equipped half-ton truck. Unfortunately, Phil, who had done so much to organize the day, was unable to come with us. Some unexpected repairs needed to be done on the roof of his house that day.

Whitney Nostalgia Tour, Algonquin Park, 1999. From left to right: Alex MacGregor, Felix Voldock, John Craftchick, Ernie Gorgerat, Carl Dubreuil, Fred Kmith, Don McRae, Greg Larochelle, Murray McGuey, Florian Kuiack, Maxie Shalla, Dick Darrow, Andrew Sydock.

After we had boarded the bus, I explained what we intended to do and where we were going. I was a little nervous as these men had known me only as a young man new to the job. Now they were being taken off into the wilderness by a much older stranger.

The nervousness disappeared shortly after the driver started up the bus. That is when the banter, laughter, and stories began and they didn't stop until we returned around four. We talked and laughed about "the boss," Dunc, Paddy, Sandy, and many others—it was great. I told the story about Tommy Cannon serving me up his eggs and how much Dunc had enjoyed that. Most had not heard that one.

Bill Hubbert had selected several sites to look at, each representing a different forest condition, and provided well-illustrated handouts outlining the history of harvesting and silvicultural operations in the areas. A disc cut from a maple tree showed the dramatic growth of residual trees following a partial removal of crop trees. In his usual manner, he clearly explained the science of modern forest-management methods. The men all understood the explanation and were favourably impressed with the changes in the forest since they had last been there.

At one point, I was walking back to the bus with Maxie Shalla. He was shaking his head in amazement and said, "We cut in this area over forty years ago. Now, the timber is younger and of better quality than it was then. When we finished cutting, I couldn't see any future for the bush. Now I can, and it feels good."

We stopped at the bridge over the outlet of Lake Louisa to enjoy Elva's lunch. All except Felix Voldock, who was in his early nineties at the time. He told us, "I only eat two small meals a day and sometimes just one. I never eat lunch. Today, men eat and sit around too much and that is why they are dropping like flies in their fifties and sixties."

As a few of us walked up the road a piece to stretch, I noticed an old fellow standing quietly in a small clearing not far from the lake. It was the same spot where "Hay Lake" Joe, Eddie, and I had parked our truck the day we fought with the stone. When I went over to him, he pointed to the opening and told me, "I was operating a bulldozer when McRae first built this road back in the late 1950s. There was an old horse stable right there, and my helper and I batched it here for a couple of weeks. You might say that there was no room at the inn," he added with a big grin.

As we were driving toward Harry Lake, where we would turn around to come back, Fred Kmith pointed out the window in the direction of a nice stand of maple trees. He informed us that, "Just over that hill in the middle of all those maples, there is an apple tree. Some of us were having lunch on a log landing one day and Fred Parks, who had an apple in his lunch, planted a seed. Believe it or not, it grew. It probably has a couple of sixteen-foot sawlogs in the butt by now. It may have already gone through McRae's sawmill. Too bad it is so far away or we could go and have a look."

On our return trip we stopped the bus at the Rock Lake mill site. A few of us got out and walked around the planted red pines. The men walked silently near the former garage and cookery, once in a while kicking the ground to see if there was a chunk of chain or an artifact that could be taken home as a souvenir. It reminded me of scenes of World War II veterans returning to stroll the beaches of Normandy, each one with his own thoughts. I know I had mine, and they were good ones!

When we arrived back in Whitney, pictures were taken of the group beside the bus and we said our farewells for the last time. Just as Bill and I were leaving, Fred Kmith invited us up to his place to see the collection of axe heads he had on display in his workshop.

It was more than a collection. It was a veritable axe museum, representing years of Fred rummaging around the remains of old logging camps. The workshop walls were covered with broad axes, scoring axes, felling axes and, believe it or not, a two-man axe. Fred had a story for every axe and hard work was stamped on each one. It was a marvellous way to end a super day.

Shortly after the nostalgia tour, Maxie Shalla suddenly passed away. On my way through Whitney one day, I stopped in to see his wife Stella to offer her my condolences. She described how thrilled Maxie was that evening when he came home from our tour. He frequently talked about the day with his family and many friends. It is a nice feeling to know that we were able to take Maxie back into Algonquin Park one last time.

On a Saturday night in March 2000 in the Pembroke Catering Hall, the curtain closed on my formal career in forestry. Behind me, now, were the close relationships with all the amazing people who have passed my way. It was now time for Heather and me to embark on our retirement career. Perhaps there would be time to write a book. The tributes and gifts were beautiful and much appreciated. I was especially pleased to have withstood the roasting, as well as get in my own licks at some deserving subjects.

As I looked out over the smiling faces of friends, colleagues, and family, my emotions were mainly of gratitude. There were happy expectations of the days to come, interspersed with the occasional tinge of sadness. My parents were too frail to attend but, as I told the gathering that night, they were content to be at home in Lachute, Quebec, keeping an eye on separatist Lucien Bouchard.

I thought of those who had passed on before: Mansiel Wilson, Jack McRae, Duncan MacGregor, and many others. I had a special salute for Joe Bird in my mind. He had touched my life and had been the one who had enough faith in me to bring me back to Algonquin Park to fulfill a boyhood dream.

Johnnie Shaw wasn't there, but I wasn't surprised at that. We had already said farewell, and he didn't like celebrations. Besides, he probably had some WHMIS signs to put up. Young John and Dana told me later that he had intended to come, but had ended up by mistake at the Best Western hotel, after which he returned home. He wasn't about to be driving around Pembroke all night looking for a party.

I felt many sentiments that night. Probably the most memorable and emotional one of the evening was when our youngest daughter Nancy went to the podium to say a few words on behalf of our family. She gave a perspective that I had really not thought about much before.

She explained that when she and her brothers and sisters get together, they often reminisce about their good times at home. They recall how happy I was with my job and that I always seemed to be enthusiastic about going to work in the morning. She went on to explain, however, that my exuberance was not always shared by the kids, especially when I banged on bedroom doors in the morning shouting, "Rise and shine, it's daylight in the swamp."

Yes, indeed, I had been very happy in my work. How could I not, having worked a lifetime in such a special sanctuary as Algonquin Park and having shared bologna sandwiches and gallons of tea with all these remarkable people you have met.

Brent A. Connelly

**Holy Old
Whistlin'**

138

I have had a good run. And now, as I sign off and go to the closet to make sure the bush boots are still there beside the golf clubs, I repeat my favourite prescription for "the gift of life":

"Count your life by smiles not tears, count your age by friends not years!"

References

Corbett, Ron. *The Last Guide*. Penguin Books Canada Ltd.

MacGregor, Roy. *A Life in the Bush—lessons from my father*. Penguin Books Canada Ltd.

Shaw-Cullen, Lisbeth and Lisa Shaw-Verhoek. *A Celebration of Herb Shaw and Sons Ltd. 1847–1997*. Shaw-Verhoek.

Strickland, Dan. *Barron Canyon Trail*. The Friends of Algonquin.

Townsend, Ray. *Field Notes and Diary Entries*. Unpublished.

Townsend, Ray. *Algonquin Forestry Authority . . . A 20 Year History (1975–1995)*. The Algonquin Forestry Authority.

— *Algonquin Logging Museum*. Co-operative Development: The Ontario Ministry of Natural Resources, The Friends of Algonquin, and The Algonquin Forestry Authority.

— *Bits & Pieces*. The Economic Press Inc.

— *The Eganville Leader—Reflections of a Century*. The Eganville Leader.

Photo Credits: Ray Townsend, Walter Dombroski, The Algonquin Forestry Authority, Bob McRae, Heather Draycroft, Tommy Clouthier, Carl Corbett, Bob Pick, Dana Shaw, Jeff Driscoll.

Acknowledgements

For the most part, this book was written with my family and friends knowing nothing about it. I like to think of it as being the ultimate Christmas stocking stuffer for them, while at the same time giving me an opportunity to acknowledge the many amazing people I worked with in Algonquin Park.

I am extremely grateful to author Roy MacGregor for suggesting that I write a book in the first place and for his ongoing encouragement and advice. I am especially indebted to my wife Heather and our daughter Nancy for their support and guidance. They are also to be commended for keeping the secret.

A book is never a book until it is a book. Up until the time it is published, it is only a manuscript and, for many first-time authors like myself, maybe gathering dust in some dark cupboard. I have Tim Gordon, publisher at General Store Publishing House, to thank for walking on the edge in his decision to publish Holy Old Whistlin'. Special mention also goes out to members of his capable team, namely, designer Tara Yourth and publicist Ann Forgie.

My deepest appreciation is extended to a true editing professional, General Store senior editor Susan Code McDougall, who after reading an early draft told me that I was long-winded and unfocused, and threw commas around like raisins in a cake. And we went from there. There is no doubt that meeting Susan was the turning point for me. Readers can judge if she was successful in pointing me in the right direction. She certainly tried.

Finally, my heart is filled with gratitude for Jack McRae, Donald McRae, and Joe Bird for fulfilling my dream when they hired me to work in Algonquin Park. God bless them!

About the Author

Brent Connelly was raised in the lower Ottawa Valley town of Brownsburg, Quebec. After obtaining his Bachelor of Science degree in Forestry from the University of New Brunswick in 1961, he began a nearly four-decade career in forestry, most of it spent in Algonquin Park. In 1975, Brent was one of the first foresters hired to work for the newly established Algonquin Forestry Authority and, over the next twenty-five years until his retirement, he held the positions of area supervisor, operations manager, and acting general manager.

Brent is a long-time member of the Ontario Professional Foresters Association and, in 2000, he received the Friends of Algonquin Directors' Award in recognition of a career dedicated to the enhancement of Algonquin Park values.

Today, Brent and his wife Heather reside in Ottawa where they can frequently be seen skating on the canal or gliding along city bike trails. They have seven children and eleven grandchildren. Brent had so much fun with *Holy Old Whistlin'*, his first book, that he may consider another book to capture the spirit of the rugged Algoma loggers that he worked with in Lake Superior Park.

One more thing: Buried in *Holy Old Whistlin'* is an outrageous and impossible description of a logging tool. The author would be interested in hearing from any readers who find it. The first one to do so will be treated to a bush lunch on the shores of Lake Travers in Algonquin Park. It will consist of a toasted baloney, cheddar cheese, and onion sandwich on homemade bread washed down with black tea made from loose tea leaves, with a six-inch date square for dessert.

To order more copies of

Contact:
GENERAL STORE
PUBLISHING HOUSE
499 O'Brien Road, Box 415
Renfrew, Ontario Canada K7V 4A6
Telephone: 1-800-465-6072
Fax: (613) 432-7184
www.gsph.com

VISA and MASTERCARD accepted.